The Addicted Brain

The Addicted Brain

Why We Abuse
Drugs, Alcohol, and Nicotine

Michael Kuhar

Vice President, Publisher: Tim Moore
Associate Publisher and Director of Marketing: Amy Neidlinger
Acquisitions Editor: Tim Moore
Editorial Assistant: Pamela Boland
Development Editor: Russ Hall
Operations Specialist: Jodi Kemper
Senior Marketing Manager: Julie Phifer
Assistant Marketing Manager: Megan Graue
Cover Designer: Chuti Prasertsith
Managing Editor: Kristy Hart
Project Editor: Jovana San Nicolas-Shirley
Copy Editor: Ginny Bess Munroe
Proofreader: Kathy Ruiz
Senior Indexer: Cheryl Lenser
Senior Compositor: Gloria Schurick
Manufacturing Buyer: Dan Uhrig

© 2012 by Pearson Education, Inc.

Upper Saddle River, New Jersey 07458

For information about buying this title in bulk quantities, or for special sales opportunities (which may include electronic versions; custom cover designs; and content particular to your business, training goals, marketing focus, or branding interests), please contact our corporate sales department at corpsales@pearsoned.com or (800) 382-3419.

For government sales inquiries, please contact governmentsales@pearsoned.com.

For questions about sales outside the U.S., please contact international@pearsoned.com.

Company and product names mentioned herein are the trademarks or registered trademarks of their respective owners.

Printed in the United States of America

Fourth Printing: March 2014

ISBN-10: 0-13-428858-0
ISBN-13: 978-0-13-428858-0

Pearson Education LTD.
Pearson Education Australia PTY, Limited.
Pearson Education Singapore, Pte. Ltd.
Pearson Education Asia, Ltd.
Pearson Education Canada, Ltd.
Pearson Educación de Mexico, S.A. de C.V.
Pearson Education—Japan
Pearson Education Malaysia, Pte. Ltd.

The Library of Congress cataloging-in-publication data is on file.

This product is printed digitally on demand. This book is the paperback version of an original hardcover book.

This book is dedicated to those afflicted with brain disease, to their caregivers and supporters, and to the researchers who hope for a better future.

Contents

Acknowledgments

Several individuals made important contributions to this book. I thank Dr. JoAnna Perry, who edited, contributed to several chapters, and obtained permissions for reproducing data; Sylvia Wrobel, who contributed to the first three chapters; Jordan Licata, who compiled the glossary; and Janie Langford, who helped obtain permissions.

I also thank others who contributed to the book in various ways: Jo Tunstall, Pat Harris, Brenda Lloyd, Susan Marshall, Dr. David Gorelick, Dr. Eliot Gardner, Dr. Roy Wise, Dr. Leonard Howell, Dr. Heather Kimmel, and Dr. Darryl Neill.

The editors, Russ Hall and Kirk Jensen, provided much needed advice and assistance every step of the way.

I am very grateful for my mentors, colleagues, and trainees, who, for more than four decades helped develop my skills and knowledge so that this book was possible. Support from the National Institutes of Health (NIH) was essential.

Finally, I thank the Fulbright program and colleagues at the Catholic University in Santiago, Chile, especially Dr. Katya Gysling, who helped shape this book in my mind.

About the Author

Michael Kuhar, Ph.D., is currently a professor at the Yerkes National Primate Research Center, Candler professor in the Emory University School of Medicine, and a Georgia Research Alliance Eminent Scholar. His general interests have been the structure and function of the brain, mental illness, and the drugs that affect the brain. Addiction has been his major focus for many years, and he is one of the most productive and highly cited scientists worldwide. He has trained a large cadre of students, fellows, and visitors, received a number of prestigious awards for his work, and remains involved in many aspects of addiction research and education. In June 2011, he received the Nathan B. Eddy lifetime achievement award from the College on Problems of Drug Dependence.

Introduction

Robert's friends convinced him to try crack cocaine at a senior party when he was still 17 years old. It took his head places he could only imagine, and he wanted more, more, more. Three years later, he could no longer hold a job. His teeth were loose and two had fallen out. He stole. He sold his body. He did anything for more! He had been to rehab twice and was back on the street again, and all he wanted was more.

This is a book about seduction, amazing pleasure, and a world inside your head that is both fantasy and real. This fantasy world is not easy to give up, and, like all fantasies, it can be trouble if you can't get back into the real world where you need to live, work, pay bills, and take care of loved ones. Drugs, the brain, and addiction create this dreamland of fantasy, but it can quickly turn into a hell, and it often does.

Research has taught us how drugs and other pleasures affect the brain. It turns out that drugs, gambling, Internet use, and chocolate all affect the brain in similar ways. The importance of this discovery extends well beyond knowing about drug abuse and pleasure; it impacts on ethics and morality, the nature of the brain as a survival organ, the evolution of the brain, and the good, the bad, and the ugly of human nature. Anything that reveals the vagaries and limitations of the human brain is useful and a service to us all. Understanding the brain and human behavior is a basic requirement for setting realistic goals for personal and societal improvement.

Aside from the amazing discoveries, a special glory of this book is the inclusion of wonderful techniques that help us examine the brains of drug users. For example, the development of brain imaging enables us to study how drugs affect the brain without any physical invasion of the head. This is something not even imagined decades ago. There are many other striking techniques such as drug self-administration and biochemical analyses of tissues. When I say this is a glory, I realize that reveals something about me and my preferences, but you are invited to share in this. I'm lucky that I have spent more than four decades doing this science, watching its progress, and seeing its impact on public health. Within these pages is a fascinating story of science in the service of men.

Different drugs, some legal and others illegal, release powerful demons in our brains. Surprisingly, the demons—the chemicals and nerve cells in our brains—are already there, working in an important but much smaller way that is essential for our functioning. Drugs create the demons by disrupting the chemicals and nerve cells so that they get out of control and wreak havoc in many people. Decades of scientific research have revealed how this happens.

The demons behave as expected. Once unleashed and in power, they don't go away easily. Even after we stop taking drugs, they influence our actions for a long time, for many months or even years. They want you to continue to feed them by taking more and more drugs. Part of the power of the demons is that they reside in powerful brain systems. These brain systems *have* to be powerful because they have a big job, such as keeping us fit and surviving. The long life and the power of the demons make them formidable enemies, but we are not alone or helpless. Treatment and rehab centers help us regain control of our lives. The same demons seem to apply to other addictions—gambling, carbohydrates, sex, and the Internet. Studying one addiction—drugs—helps us understand other addictions.

Knowing the demons is helpful. Because we can understand them and what they do, we can develop medications and other treatments to thwart them and help drug users. In fact, the search for medications, although not yet complete, has been quite successful. We gain ground every day. Also, changing our behaviors and habits in constructive ways thwarts the demons.

Some of us are lucky and we either have no interest in drugs or can walk away from them at any time. Everybody's brains are different, at least to some degree, and have different vulnerabilities to drug use. Surprisingly, women and men respond differently to drugs, and so do adolescents and adults. Teens are a special concern because of their youth and increased sensitivity to drugs. Many studies have revealed why this is so and why some of us are more likely to get into trouble with drugs than others. Stress, involved in so many health problems, also feeds the demons of drug abuse. Our genetics also play a role, but not an overwhelming one; we can still fight back.

Drug abuse and addiction are costly, not the least because of the misery they bring. Because of this cost, society has invested in science to combat drug use. It is paying off. We have found the demons, and we can fight. But if you are new to the war itself, because of the addiction of a loved one, a patient, or yourself, then prepare to arm yourself to fight.

1

What's in This Book, and Why Should I Read It?

"I'm only 14 years old and I'm in a drug counselor's office. I've been stealing, missing school, and failing most of my subjects. It seemed to start when I got involved with drugs. We got dope from older brothers and sisters, from parents' medicine cabinets, and on the streets. We never thought of it as 'doing drugs.' We were just having fun and hanging out, and we thought we could stop anytime. But we fooled ourselves. It caught up to us big time. Now I need to find out about what happened and what I can do to turn my life around. I need to know everything!"

Getting hooked on drugs is a sequence of attraction, seduction, compulsion, and pain. Drugs are dangerous and widespread, and dealing with them requires knowledge and help. This book is about alcohol, nicotine, and illegal drugs—how they work, what they do to the brain, and what can be done to stop using them. The book is especially about what happens inside the brain and why the brain just happens to be set up for drugs. Yes, the brain is set up for drugs; the brain is a co-conspirator, albeit an unwitting one!

When is someone a drug abuser or an addict?[1] If someone uses drugs casually and infrequently without significant problems and can take them or leave them, that person might best be called a *user*, which is still a dangerous situation. If taking drugs causes significant distress and problems in the person's life, then *abuser* might be the best descriptor. If drugs are in control of a person's life, or if they can't stop, or if they do drugs in spite of personal distress and negative consequences, then they might be drug *dependent* or *addicted*. Even people who are not users, abusers, or addicts are very likely to gain from reading this book.

The text box that follows provides definitions of specific levels of drug use. Addiction is the most serious form of the disorder[2] and it can develop when drugs are taken repeatedly over a long period of time. Taking larger quantities of drugs more frequently is likely to result in addiction more quickly. However, there is no mathematical equation describing this process. It is not exact. Moreover, the process varies depending on the individual and his or her circumstances.

Definitions

DSM IV TR is the latest edition of the *Diagnostic and Statistical Manual of Mental Disorders* that is published through the American Psychiatric Association. It is the official manual for defining and diagnosing the spectrum of disorders that involve drug use. It is used by professionals to more precisely define the degree of drug abuse. Please see this manual for the official definitions.[3]

- **Drug use** can refer to any use of a drug, but more often, it refers to an occasional or recreational use of drugs. In this case, acute or immediate effects and toxicities can be significant. If the drug used is an illegal one, then there is the legal transgression to be concerned with, too. Also, there is the danger of continued use of drugs to where they become a more serious problem.

- **Drug abuse** is a more serious problem where there is a greater degree of drug use and a distressing or negative impact on the drug user's life. It can get further out of control.

- **Addiction** or **dependence** is yet more serious and includes more of a loss of control over drug seeking and drug taking in spite of distress and/or negative consequences. Note that both loss of control over behavior and distress or negative consequences are emphasized. But, there are additional characteristics of drug addiction that are well known. Considerable time may be spent getting and using the drug. More drug is taken than intended. Efforts to stop taking the drug often fail. Tolerance, which is the need to take larger quantities of the drug to get the same effect, develops. Also, perhaps there are withdrawal symptoms when the effect of the drug wears off. Thus, an individual might have a problem with drugs even though there are no distressing feelings or negative consequences that are evident. The words addiction or dependence are used to refer to more severe cases of drug seeking and taking.

The use of drugs is not simply a passing fad or the latest, cool thing. Drugs of one type or another have been with us for a long time, literally thousands of years. Opium has been used in China for centuries, and cocaine use in early Indian cultures goes back centuries. There is even a reference in the Bible about getting drunk on wine. There are things about both the nature of drugs and the human brain that make drug use enduring over the ages, and this reveals a special vulnerability in humans. For example, in 2006-2007 in the United States, there were more than 22 million people, 12 years of age and older, who were classified with drug abuse or drug dependence on illicit drugs[4] or alcohol.

What is it about addiction that grips certain individuals so firmly that they lose at least some control over their drug taking and sometimes over their lives? This book attempts to answer this question by examining research discoveries from the previous couple of decades. Extraordinary progress has been made in drug abuse research.

What Is a Drug?

When talking about drugs that can be abused, there are about seven different groups of substances. These are nicotine; sedatives such as alcohol, barbiturates, benzodiazepines, and inhalants such as fumes from glue; opiates such as heroin and morphine; psychostimulants such as cocaine, amphetamine, and methamphetamine; marijuana; hallucinogens; and caffeine. Prescription drugs that are abused comprise many of the previous classes and are shown in the following list:

- Club drugs, which includes:
  - GHB (Also known as Goop)
  - Ketamine (Also known as K)
  - MDMA (Also known as E)
  - Rohypnol (Also known as Roofies)
- Cocaine, which is also known as nose candy, C, and blow
- Crack (another form of cocaine, and also known as Freebase, Rooster, and Tornado)
- Hallucinogens, which includes:
  - LSD
  - Mescaline (cactus)
  - Psilocybin (Mexican mushrooms)
- Heroin (Also known as Big H, China White, and Smack)
- Inhalants, which include:
  - Air blast
  - Huffing
  - Moon gas
- Marijuana
- Methamphetamine (Also known as Crank, Ice, and Stove top)
- Prescription drugs, which include:
  - Methaqualone (Also known as Ludes)
  - Oxycontin (Also known as Hillbilly heroin)
  - Ritalin (Also known as Vitamin R)
- Steroids (Also known as Juice, Pumpers, and Weight trainers)

This list is composed of illicit drugs and doesn't include alcohol or nicotine. A much more detailed list of abused drugs can be found on the ONDCP (Office of National Control Drug Policy) website at http://www.whitehousedrugpolicy.gov/drugfact/crack/index.html.

Why are *these* groups of chemicals addicting? It is striking how they can have such different effects and uses; for example, opiates relieve pain, and sedatives produce sleep, yet both have the danger of addiction. What is it about these chemicals, and not others, that give them such power? A reasonable answer is that it is an *accident* that all these particular compounds are addicting. There are, perhaps, millions of chemical compounds on this earth, and it is, perhaps, just unfortunate that some of these chemicals can hook into the brain in such a way that they become addicting. Of course, some of these drugs are used more than others (see Figure 1-1).

It is useful and can eliminate confusion to make a distinction between the words *drugs* and *medications*. The word *drug* is used in this book to refer to a substance with the potential to cause harm, abuse, and addiction. Of course, there are other drugs that are therapeutic, cure diseases, and are employed by doctors to treat specific maladies. These latter substances are referred to herein as *medications*. Drugs of abuse can also have legitimate uses in medicine and be medications. Cocaine is a powerful vasoconstrictor in that it closes off blood vessels and can be used to reduce bleeding in surgery. Amphetamine is a stimulant and can be used to treat Attention Deficit Hyperactivity Disorder (ADHD). Opiates are indispensable in the treatment of pain, but they can cause addiction nonetheless. Depending on how and why they are used, many of the substances can be both drugs *and* medications. *Prescription drugs* are another example of this; they are medications that can be abused and therefore are also drugs.

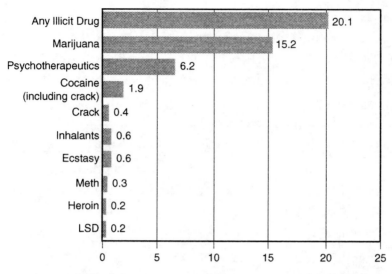

Figure 1-1   The number of individuals, ages 12 or older, who have used the indicated drug within the past 12 months (in millions). Psychotherapeutics refers to prescription drugs that were abused; these drugs include Oxycontin, Vicodin, amphetamines, Ritalin, and sedatives. These numbers of users, which range from 200,000 to over 15 million, are small compared to the number of individuals using the legal drugs, like alcohol and nicotine. More than 50 million people smoke, and an even larger number take alcohol regularly. The relatively larger use of alcohol and nicotine are probably due to the legality of these drugs and their greater availability. Legal drugs are used probably ten times more than illicit ones. (Source: SAMSHA, 2008, National Survey on Drug Use and Health, September 2009).

Why People Take Drugs

People take drugs for many reasons. They can produce a so-called rush of pleasurable sensations, which is a dramatic and memorable experience. Sometimes drugs are taken because of peer pressure or stress. Related to the latter, drugs are sometimes used to self-medicate unpleasant feelings such as pain, anxiety, or depression. When addicted, users may take drugs to avoid the negative symptoms of withdrawal. Withdrawal is a series of distressing feelings and physiologic reactions that occur when drug taking is stopped.

The Drug Experience

The drug experience usually fits a pattern among users. The first use of a drug, a critical occurrence, is often influenced by various factors that include curiosity, friends who may apply pressure to try a drug, availability of a drug, or even a permissive home where parents and siblings are users. Reactions to a drug can vary among individuals. Some people enjoy them and some don't. Perhaps someone begins taking a medication for a medical problem such as pain and then continues using.

The next phase is persistent drug use, in which there is more individual initiative and drive to find and take drugs. This can result in problems such as chronic intoxication, missing work or school, and perhaps stealing. There might be other missed obligations, arrests, or irresponsible behaviors such as unprotected sex. If drug taking continues, a state of addiction can result. Also, more and more of a drug may be taken to get the same effect, and efforts to stop drug use may fail. Other drug-related problems can occur in life, and good health can be threatened. Although some people can stop using drugs, others drift in and out of drug use for decades or for a lifetime. Someone might someday find that his or her life is gone, wasted by a brain disorder that he or she failed to understand and cope with.

Some drug abusers are lucky; they can quit by themselves or find a family member, friend, or counselor who can help them stop. They might get into treatment on their own or they might be forced into treatment by a judge. However it happens, treatment is effective, even for people forced into it. Sadly, because of ignorance, poverty, denial, or fear of the stigma of being labeled an addict, some never find treatment.

Drug Use Is Costly in Many Ways

Many individuals and families know from first-hand experience how hurtful addiction can be, not only to the drug users, but also to individuals around them. The consequences of drug use include damaging families, relationships, or communities, and perhaps increasing the risks for serious illness or crime. Often, the drug user has vowed to stop and has tried to stop many times only to fall back and relapse into further drug use or dependence. The resulting feelings of helplessness, impotence, and failure can engulf and doom someone's entire world.

The personal and societal costs of drugs can be seen around us and in the media. Robert Downey Jr., a well known actor, producer, and singer, had a serious problem with drugs. He described to a judge how he couldn't stop using them even though he knew he was in trouble. He also said that while starring on the television series Ally McBeal, he was at a low point and didn't care if his acting career was over. But after five years of drug abuse, arrests, stints in rehab, and many relapses, he settled down to work on his problem. Ray Charles, the legendary performer, was addicted to heroin, but after his third drug bust, he went into rehab and gave up the drug. Fortunately, there are individuals who generously come forward, tell us their stories, and warn us about drugs. But not all drug users accept treatment or stop taking drugs, and that group generates great concern. There is even greater concern when our peers or the media glamorize drug use, which is quite dangerous.

Drug abuse is expensive. When we include additional health care costs, productivity losses, costs of crime, and so on, the dollar amount is great.[5] In 2002, for example, overall costs exceeded 180 billion dollars, and loss of productivity accounted for a large portion of that (see Figure 1-2). Costs increased more than 5 percent annually since 1992, with the most rapid increase in costs related to the criminal justice system. These dollar figures are comparable to those for heart disease, cancer, and mental illness. They reflect a major drain on society's resources. Of course, dollar amounts do not begin to reflect the *misery* that drug use can create for the individual, his or her friends, and family.

While the problems are great, they are not hopeless. Perhaps determination is wanting. Dr. Bertha Madras, a Harvard researcher in drug addiction and a former White House official, says, "When viewed from a national perspective, the drug abuse problem in this country is staggering. Yet I am certain that we can develop effective solutions and strategies if we overcome our biggest challenge—finding resolve."

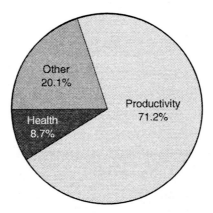

Figure 1-2   Distribution of illicit drug costs in 2002 by major components. The largest fraction of the cost of drug abuse is due to loss of productivity. "Other" costs primarily reflect the costs of the criminal justice system (incarceration, court costs, and so on) costs to victims of related crimes, and costs for social welfare. From source cited in note 5.

Other Addictions

Although this is a book about drugs and how people become hooked on drugs, it is also about *all* of our appetites; therefore, it can help us understand other potential addictions such as eating and gambling. For example, if someone overeats, craves carbohydrates every day, and has withdrawal symptoms when he stops cold turkey, then he may have a problem with carbohydrates. If such a person seeks help, then this book can help with understanding the problem and the needs for treatment. More is said later about food, gambling, and sexual drives.

Other Medications

Another point is that some therapeutically useful medicines (not addicting drugs), such as antidepressants, need to be taken over long periods of time and should not be stopped abruptly because of the danger of recurring disease. Studies of abused drugs, which also involve taking drugs over a long period of time, can inform us not only about how the useful medications produce their beneficial actions in the brain, but also about the problems in abruptly stopping their use.

Brain Structure and Functions

Before embarking on a study of the addicted brain, it is necessary to be aware of the brain and its organization. Different parts of the brain have different functions. Seventy-five percent of the human brain is made up of the wrinkled outer covering referred to as the cerebral cortex, which has different functional areas. Strokes or lesions of the motor cortex result in paralysis, the extent of which is dependent on the extent of the motor area involved. Patients with strokes in the association cortex have deficits of perception and attention. When the temporal lobe is damaged, the ability to recognize or name objects is impaired. Lesions or strokes of the frontal lobe result in personality changes, planning deficits, and inabilities to carry out complex behaviors. Strokes or tumors in other parts of the brain have many other effects as well (see Figure 1-3).

The brain is also the organ of awareness. When general anesthetics are administered, the electrical activity of the brain is reduced, and we lose awareness or go to sleep. If we stimulate the visual cortex, we might have visual images pop into our awareness. If the olfactory cortex is stimulated, then we might perceive odors. If we stimulate other parts of the brain, other events or sensations enter our awareness. Emotional behavior is also based in the brain. A group of brain regions collectively known as the limbic system controls emotional behavior and is partly responsible for feeling good. The following chapters link certain brain regions with feeling good and with drugs.

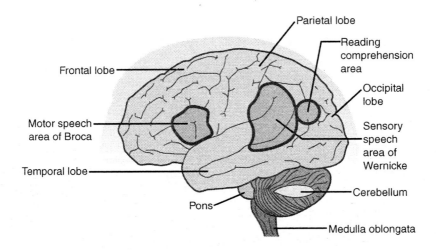

Figure 1-3　A lateral (sideways) surface view of the brain shows some of the more obvious regions, and each region has its own function. The specific functions of the various brain regions have become known after centuries of studies of patients with strokes, injuries, and tumors. Drug addiction also involves certain regions. (Adapted from http://medicalimages.allrefer.com/large/brain.jpg, accessed on December 20, 2010.)

The Tool Box

Science, like everything else in our lives, has become technology-driven, and there are marvelous new approaches and instruments that allow us to examine the tiniest parts of our chromosomes or peer into the depths of our brains without surgical invasion of the skull. These tools are powerful and interesting in and of themselves.

The science of genetics has advanced, and it is now possible, with a small sample of blood, to examine our genes. Because genes are the basis of heredity, and some aspects of drug addiction are heritable, studies of genes can be informative. The target of these studies is DNA, which is made up of four different chemicals called bases, and it is *the order of these chemicals in our DNA* that specifies our genes. These chemicals—abbreviated as the letters A, T, G, and C—are lined up in two parallel strands that comprise the structure of DNA. Again, it is the sequence of these bases, in groups of three, that constitutes our genetic code, and certain parts of our genetic code can contribute to the likelihood of our becoming a drug user.

For looking inside our brains, noninvasive brain imaging techniques can be astonishing. Magnetic resonance imaging (or MRI) describes the structure of our brains, such that changes in the size of parts of our brains can be measured. Functional magnetic resonance imaging (fMRI) tells us about the functional activity of various brain regions. Positron emission tomography (PET) scanning is versatile. It can be used to reveal the activity of different brain regions or even the levels of certain brain chemicals and proteins. Overall, genetic and imaging studies are but two of the new tools that have become available over the past 25 to 35 years. These tools are out in front in the attack on drugs.

Questions to Be Answered

This book addresses many questions about drugs and the brain, including:

- Why is it said that addiction is a brain disorder rather than perhaps a moral failing?
- What happens in the brain of someone who uses drugs repeatedly?
- Can better medications for addicted individuals be expected in the future?
- Why is drug abuse chronic and relapsing, which is part of the essence of this disorder?
- Why are drugs so powerful that they can gain control of our behaviors, but we can't give up responsibility for our actions?
- Will *I* become drug dependent?
- Are there differences among, men, women, adolescents, and older adults in how they respond to and experience drugs?
- Can one recover from drug addiction and be cured?
- The stigma of being a drug abuser is a problem in that it often prevents searching for treatment or dealing with the problem openly.

Endnotes

[1] Throughout this book, we tend to refer to addiction as a disorder, but it is also often called a disease. The definition of addiction that is used in this book focuses on continued drug use in spite of distress and negative consequences. However, the official description is given in the Diagnostic and Statistical Manual of Mental Disorders produced by the American Psychiatric Association, and it includes more elements. The DSM IV TR is the current edition used by medical professionals for official diagnoses. The DSM is an evolving document and DSM V is due in the near future. Currently, the diagnosis of drug dependence requires the presence of three or more of several symptoms, and it is possible to have a diagnosis of substance dependence without the presence of distress or negative consequences. The official list of symptoms and diagnostic criteria for Substance Dependence and Substance Abuse can be found in an online version of the DSM IV TR. One possible site is http://www.psychiatryonline.com/content.aspx?aID=629, which was accessed on June 28, 2011. Only a qualified professional can make a diagnosis.

[2] Ibid.

[3] Ibid.

[4] An illicit drug is one that is not legal to produce, not legal to use or possess, or a medically useful therapeutic drug that is used non-medically.

[5] Office of National Drug Control Policy (2004). "The Economic Costs of Drug Abuse in the United States," 1992–2002. Washington, DC: Executive Office of the President (Publication No. 207303).

2

Hardwired: What Animals Tell Us About the Human Desire for Drugs

"I gotta get a hit. I steal money, leave work in the middle of the day to get high, and I can't stop. What's happened to me?"

For many years, doctors and scientists have been trying to figure out how addiction works and how addicts can be treated. The research has become sophisticated with elaborate laboratories for human subjects in many of our best medical centers. Hundreds and hundreds of publications every year describe new findings that promise a better understanding of and improved treatments for drug abusers.

Studies with animals, in addition to humans, have been helpful. In fact, using animals in research has a number of advantages over studying humans.[1] Importantly, the environment, nutrition, general health, and drug use of an animal can be rigidly controlled since its birth, although this is not possible with humans. Because of this, animal experiments can be more carefully defined and more easily interpreted. Also, animals cannot refuse good medical care during periods of experimentation, whereas humans are not bound to follow medical advice. Animals are in controlled and protected environments, whereas we have little control over humans' choices of environments. In addition, animals can be given new treatments and medications, and indeed, the FDA requires that animals be used for proof of safety of new medications. Despite these advantages, the use of animals in research is not taken without care or caution. Each and every experimental procedure must be described in detail and approved by a learned committee before the experiments can be carried out.[2] Unexpected problems are studied by committees to learn how we can better care for our animal subjects. Scientists are sensitive to these issues and often have beloved pets at home.

Going Back for More

Although animals were part of addiction research during the 1920s, this earlier research focused primarily on understanding how drugs affected the animal's physiology. Typically, drugs were injected into animals that were held or immobilized; the animals were passive recipients. Then a variety of tests and measurements were made on the animals, and a great deal was learned that is the basis of much work today. But in a new procedure developed in the 60s and 70s, the animals were given control over their own drug injections. They actively and freely pressed a lever to get a drug injection. The rate of lever pressing reflected their desire for more of the drug and its effects. This control over drug taking is more like the situation with humans who have control over drug taking and provides a better animal model of human drug taking.

This procedure or model was developed by several scientists including Drs. James Weeks, C.R. Schuster, and Tomoji Yanagita. When animals were allowed to administer drugs to themselves by pressing a lever, they did so, and with surprising gusto! In this drug self-administration model, a catheter is placed surgically under anesthesia in an animal's jugular vein so that a measured quantity of a drug can be delivered (by a lever press) directly to the animal's bloodstream where it rapidly circulates to the brain. The animals appear to quickly adapt to the presence of the catheter, going about their activities probably with no more notice than a dog pays to his or her leash while out on a walk.

There are small variations on how to do this, but the idea is that an animal is placed in a sound-insulated chamber to avoid distraction and is then presented with two levers. One activates delivery of a saline solution, the other a saline solution containing a drug such as cocaine. Of course, the animal does not know it is receiving an injection, but it obviously learns that pressing the drug-related lever produces a different sensation than pressing the saline-related lever. Which lever it presses and how often it does so are clear, quantifiable measures of which sensation it prefers (see Figure 2-1).

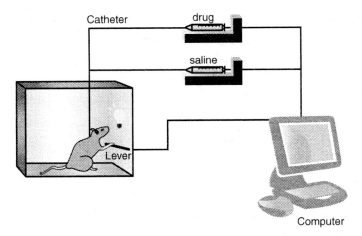

Figure 2-1   Animals will self-administer drugs. The figure shows a rat that has access to levers (only one is visible), and each lever is hooked to either saline (a saltwater solution) or a drug solution such as one with cocaine. The rat also has a catheter or drug delivery tube implanted in its blood vessels. The computer controls how often and how much of the drug is given when the lever is pressed. When the drug-related lever is pressed, the rat does not know it is getting an injection, but rather it has a sensation, and if it likes the sensation, it will press the lever again and again and again. Moreover, the rat learns to ignore the lever that results in an injection of a drug-free solution. This animal model of drug self-administration is vitally important for research and understanding the how and why of addiction. (Modified from www.pharmaco.umontreal.ca/apropos/LaboFilep/images/Self-administrationEN_000.jpg, as accessed on February 24, 2009.)

When offered one of almost any of the drugs that humans abuse (exceptions being those that distort sensations and perceptions, such as hallucinogens like LSD), the animal almost always chooses the lever that results in drug delivery. The sensation brought about by the infusion of the drug is positive and acts as a *reward* that positively *reinforces* the act of pressing the lever. Every lever press, followed by an infusion of the sensation-producing drug, further reinforces the lever-pressing behavior. The animal appears hooked, pressing the lever repeatedly. In the case of a rewarding drug, such as cocaine, the animal might ignore food, water, or even a sexually available mate, and it presses the lever until it is too exhausted to continue. Although the animal controls the act of lever pressing, the researcher controls the total amount of drug that is administered and prevents the animal from taking enough to injure or kill itself accidentally, as sadly can happen with humans.

If the researcher suddenly reverses the levers so that the one delivering cocaine now delivers saline, the animal soon discovers the drug-related lever and starts pressing it. If the drug is removed completely, the animal keeps lever pressing for some time, apparently in the hope that it will reappear. It might require a large number of unsuccessful presses to "extinguish" the pressing behavior, meaning the animal no longer associates pressing the lever with the desirable sensation and stops.

In these controlled experiments described previously, the animals have access to a restricted amount of drug over a restricted time. But the human situation doesn't always work that way. Sometimes drug users have access to a drug for a long, extended time. George Koob, his colleagues, and others[3] studied this in animals. They allowed some animals to have longer access to the drug. For example, rats were allowed to self-administer cocaine for either one hour or six hours per day. In the group with one hour access, cocaine intake was lower and stable over days. But the group that had six hours of access gradually *increased* its intake over days. Access and availability of a drug can make a difference in the amount of drug that is taken. This is consistent with the behavior of heavy drug users.

Because the drug self-administration paradigm has been so successful, it is a trusted model for human addiction. It is used to determine if new drugs or medications are potentially addicting. For example, if some compound X affects the brain, it is reasonable to see if it is self-administered. If it is, then it has to be considered as a potentially dangerous and addicting substance.

Because of the robust self-administration of drugs in both animals and humans, there seems no other explanation than the fact that animals and humans share some property in the brain that makes the sensation produced by these drugs desirable. In other words, there seems to be some hardwiring in the brain that is shared by both humans and animals that facilitates drug addiction. The danger of addiction is a biological vulnerability that both humans and animals share. Some see this as evidence that widespread drug-using behavior in humans cannot be simply explained as a moral weakness because a biological basis for it exists.

Darwin Saw It

Looking back, it shouldn't be surprising that at least some animals share an interest in drugs with humans. In 1871, Darwin made some interesting observations that are humorous and enlightening.

On Booze, Men, and Monkeys

"Many kinds of monkeys have a strong taste for tea, coffee, and spirituous liquors: They will also, as I have myself seen, smoke tobacco with pleasure. Brehm asserts that the natives of northeastern Africa catch the wild baboons by exposing vessels with strong beer, by which they are made drunk. He has seen some of these animals, which he kept in confinement in this state, and he gives a laughable account of their behaviors and strange grimaces. On the following morning, they were cross and dismal;

they held their aching heads with both hands and wore a most pitiable expression. When beer or wine was offered them, they turned away with disgust, but relished the juice of lemons. An American monkey, an Ateles, after getting drunk on brandy, would never touch it again, and thus was wiser than many men." (From Charles Darwin's *On The Descent of Man*, Penguin Classics, pp. 23–24)

Today Google, YouTube, and other websites permit all of us to see what our forefathers must have noted in nature: wallabies munching opium-ripe poppies, tree shrews seeking out fermented palm nectar, and even more examples of animals taking advantage of human brews carelessly left sitting around. Unfortunately for modern man, however, the attraction to alcohol, like attraction to food, can go awry in a world where both are easy to get.

Uncertain or Nonregular Rewards Are More Addicting

What if every lever press doesn't result in a drug hit, but rather about every third? As psychologists have discovered, and as any gambler knows, an occasional payoff serves as a stronger reinforcement of a given behavior than does an entirely predictable payoff.

Experiments on food reinforced behavior in the 1950s showed this nicely. Rats traversed a runway to get food as a reward. One group was given a food reward every time they moved down the runway. In another group, there was a reward only about 30 percent of the time. Both groups learned to run down the runway in expectation of a reward. Then the food reward was eliminated for both groups, but they were still allowed to run down the runway in search of it. Now you would expect that the rats wouldn't give up immediately. They would continue down the runway in subsequent trials even if they were disappointed the previous time, and that's just what they did. Now here's the interesting part. The animals that received rewards only 30 percent of the time persisted in the runway behavior much longer than the rats that were rewarded each and every time (see Figure 2-2). They tried for a longer time. A nonregular reward was more reinforcing and shaped seeking behavior more strongly than the regular reward, whereas actually, the opposite might be expected. We seem to want rewards that have been uncertain or not regular more than we do certain, regular ones!

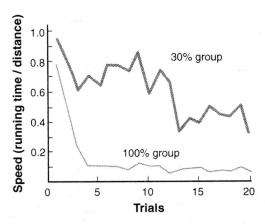

Figure 2-2   Nonregular or uncertain rewards are more addicting or reinforcing. Rats were trained to run down a runway for food. One group was rewarded with food every time, and another group was rewarded only 30 percent of the time. Then the food reward was removed completely. The group of rats that had been rewarded each and every time (100 percent of group) gave up or extinguished their running behavior more readily than the rats receiving a reward only 30 percent of the time. The 30-percent group persisted in running down the runway for longer times and more trials, even though there were no rewards. (Adapted from Figure 4.25 from *Psychology*, First Edition, by Henry Gleitman. Copyright © 1981 by W.W. Norton & Company, Inc. Used with permission of W. W. Norton & Company, Inc.)

This has important implications in our everyday life, where, for example, we may want to shape the behavior of a pet. Suppose a dog begs for table food, and you restrain yourself but nevertheless give in every so often. Although you tell yourself that you don't do it all the time, and you think you are doing well, you are in fact making it harder for the dog to stop begging. We can easily think of similar scenarios with children, students, and so on. This should give us insight into our own behaviors. Is this why some of us find gambling such a persistent urge?

Animal Model Extended

The animal model of drug self-administration (see Figure 2-1) has been critically important for research in drug addiction. Interestingly, our appreciation of the model has continued to evolve. By extending and examining the model more closely, you can study additional aspects or phases of drug addiction. These include: the initiation of drug taking or the rate at which an animal learns to self-administer it; the maintenance of drug taking, which is the phase where the lever pressing has been learned and is stable or relatively unchanging; the extinction of drug taking, which occurs when the lever pressing no longer produces a drug reward and the lever pressing gradually stops; and the relapse to drug taking, which is either stress, cue (see the following sidebar), or drug-induced, and occurs when an extinguished subject begins to seek drugs again. These four phases are different and can rely on different processes in the brain. Moreover, certain medications can be more effective in treating one phase compared to the other phases. Thus, the tools for searching for medications and treatments are becoming more sophisticated.

A "cue," in this context, is anything that reminds you of drugs or taking drugs. It can be the sight of a friend that you take drugs with, the place where you have taken drugs, or even something like a white powder whether it is drug or not. The importance of a cue is that it can precipitate a relapse. A cue can trigger a response in your brain that makes you want drugs. Someone who wants to stop taking drugs must learn his or her cues, or danger signs, that lead to craving and more drug taking, and he or she must avoid them or neutralize them in his or her mind.

An Example of a New Idea

An example of how this model can be used to explore new ideas is an experiment with CART peptide that comes from the author's laboratory. CART peptide is a chemical found in brain regions that are involved in drug abuse, and the effect of CART peptide on drug taking can be explored by using this animal model. If an animal has been allowed to learn the self-administration of cocaine, it can then be forced to give up or extinguish lever pressing by requiring a very large number of lever presses to get a reward. Instead of getting a drug injection for every lever press or for every other lever press, the number of lever presses required to get just one injection of cocaine can be made so great that the animal just gives up pressing. Now, here is the key part. The drugs that the animals like better elicit more attempts to get the drug than other less desirable drugs. The number of presses that the animal makes for a drug before it gives up is a measure of how much the animal wants the drug. Suppose animals are allowed to lever press to get injections of cocaine, and they learn to expect this whenever they press the lever. By withholding the drug injection, the number of presses required before they give up lever pressing can be measured. An interesting experimental result is that if CART peptide is injected into critical brain regions, the animal gives up lever pressing *sooner* (Figure 2-3). It appears that the animal is less interested in getting a cocaine reward when it has been given CART peptide.

The bottom line of the story is that CART peptide injected into the brain can function to make cocaine less attractive. Perhaps CART peptide is part of a chemical reflex that tries to control the excess brain activity produced by cocaine, and more will be said about this in later chapters. But, wouldn't it be interesting if medications based on CART peptide could be developed to make cocaine less attractive to addicts? This last question is speculative because we need to learn much more about CART peptide before we think about treating humans, but you get the idea. There are many experiments like this using drug self-administration that generate many new ideas for additional treatments.

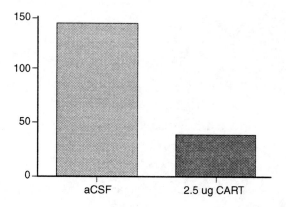

Figure 2-3   Injections of CART peptide reduce cocaine reward and intake. Animals work to receive injections of cocaine by lever pressing because they find cocaine rewarding and they want it. In fact, they press the lever many times to get a single injection of the drug. Now let's add another part to the experiment. If a drug-free solution (aCSF) is injected into the brain, the animals can still press for cocaine hoping to get some drug (the number of presses corresponds to the height of the bars in the figure). But if CART peptide (2.5 micrograms) is injected into a part of the brain associated with cocaine use (the nucleus accumbens), then the animal works much less for cocaine as indicated by the shorter bar on the right. You can think of the length of the bar as a measure of cocaine's desirability to the animal, and an injection of CART peptide reduces the desirability of cocaine and shortens the bar. More details about this kind of experiment are given in subsequent chapters. (Summarized from Jaworski et al.. "Injection of CART Peptide into the Nucleus Accumbens Reduces Cocaine Self-Administration in Rats." *Behavioral Brain Res* 191:266-271, 2008.)

You can see how important this drug self-administration model is (and other models, too). By showing that drug addiction is a physiological process based in the brain, we can then search for new medications and treatments for addiction that block or reverse the drug-induced processes in the brain. It provides a rational and physiology-based search for new treatments. We can inject drugs directly into various brain regions or surgically alter those regions to define the parts of the brain that mediate addiction. Of course, it goes without saying, that experiments like this using human beings are grossly unethical and impossible.[4] Thus, the animal models make significant progress possible.

Relapse, Craving, and Reinstatement

Drug abuse is a relapsing disorder. In fact, most drug abusers and addicts have stopped or tried to stop taking drugs, only to eventually relapse. So at any given time, most drug abusers are in fact relapsers. Therefore, it is important to study relapse itself, and this is nicely done in a variant of the self-administration model, as mentioned previously. It works by allowing the animal to learn to self-administer a drug, such as cocaine, until the lever pressing is stable. Then, the drug is withdrawn, and, as expected, the animal gradually tires of lever pressing without a reward and the lever pressing behavior is extinguished. This animal is now an experienced drug user, much like most humans who have used drugs but have stopped. A human in this condition likely thinks about the drug, and when stressed or reminded of the drug, perhaps by some cue, craves the drug and perhaps starts looking for a drug. The cue can be the sight of friends who use drugs, the crack house, or even some white powder that reminds him or her of the drug. Cues and their effects are very interesting and currently studied. For example, Drs. Leslie Lundahl and Chris-Ellyn Johanson recently found that drug-related cues set off cravings in marijuana-dependent subjects.[5] Getting even a small amount of the drug (which is a cue) might set off a binge of drug taking. So, as you can see, certain events can trigger craving, drug seeking, and relapse.

Now, let's return to the animal that has experienced a drug but is currently without it. If stress, such as a foot shock, is present or if the drug is injected, the animal remarkably starts to press the lever that previously resulted in a drug injection. The animal does this even if *no drug is given* by the lever press (see Figure 2-4). Previous drug use has conditioned the animal to look for the drug in situations that elicit cravings in humans.

In this animal model, it is possible to ask a variety of questions about relapse, and we can begin to consider which medications are best for treating or preventing relapse.

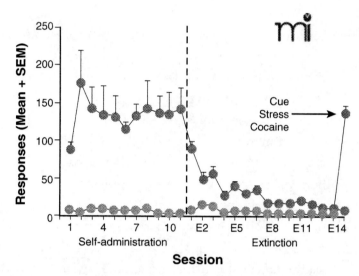

Figure 2-4   Drug self-administration in animals provides a model for relapse in humans. Animals were presented with both a drug-related lever (darker dots) and a nondrug lever (lighter dots). The nondrug lever was rarely pressed as expected (shown on the vertical axis as "responses"). They were trained for 12 days to self-administer cocaine (left half of figure), and drug delivery was accompanied by a cue, which was typically a light and/or a tone. Drug self-administration was stable at about 140 responses (on the vertical axis), except for the first day when the animals were learning. In the second phase of the experiment (right half of figure), animals underwent "extinction training" during which no drug was administered in response to lever presses (E1–E14), and the rate of lever pressing dropped nearly to zero. At the end of this second phase, animals were presented with the cue that had accompanied each drug infusion during self-administration, a mild stressor (typically foot shock), or the drug itself. Each of these stimuli reliably overcame extinction training and the animals pressed the lever, even though no drug was delivered. This reinstatement or reoccurrence of lever pressing is considered to be a bout of drug seeking or relapse. Although this is a complicated experiment, it is clear evidence that stress or a single injection of a drug can stimulate drug seeking in an animal with previous drug-taking experience. This animal model can be used to study relapse. (Adapted from PW Kalivas, Jamie Peters, and Lori Knackstedt. "Animal Models and Brain Circuits in Drug Addiction." *Mol Interv.* December 2006: 6:339–344.)

Other Animal Models

Other models allow us to study additional properties of the brain and of drugs. These models, such as "conditioned place preference" and "drug discrimination," are technical and sometimes complex but quite useful. These are mentioned only to inform you that the experimental repertoire in drug addiction research is quite rich. In the next chapter, we explore "electrical self-stimulation" and why it is important for this discussion.

A Transformation in Thinking

The realization that addiction is not only a human vulnerability but is shared by animals is important. Drug abusers were and sometimes still are considered disgusting, moral failures, hardly worthy of help, much less research programs. Their out-of-control drug seeking with its associated crimes and degradations leaves them stigmatized and sometimes abandoned. The drug abusers themselves feel helpless and hopeless. But realizing that addiction is a brain disorder, maybe like a migraine headache or a seizure, is transformative. Now we think that if we can learn enough about the brain, we can more effectively treat addicts, and this is becoming true. The drug users themselves realize that a new realm of treatment possibilities has been opened to them. These include medications and behavioral therapies directed at the brain and how it functions. This is not to say that older, existing programs are not effective. On the contrary, many are effective. However, we are now adding to the options for treatment. One of the most important functions of research is not only to make discoveries, but also to provide hope for the future and hope for treatments that are now lacking.

Summary

Animals take drugs in the same way that humans do and are considered as models for human drug use. Because studies of drugs and the brain are essential, and because many types of studies on humans are not possible, animal models have been used and have been successful.

Endnotes

[1]   Under certain, strict conditions, it is possible to carry out research with human drug abusers. The conditions of the experiments must minimize any risk to the human subject. The subjects must be physically fit and offered treatment even if they refuse it. Of course, they must be medically monitored to avoid any unsuspected and damaging effects of drugs. For example, certain doses of certain drugs that can sometimes be toxic must be avoided. Finally, every human experiment must be described in detail in writing in advance, and the description must be studied by an expert committee that can approve the experiment. The safety of human subjects is paramount, and the benefits from the research must outweigh any risks to the subjects. There are federal regulations for the protection of human research subjects (45 CFR 46, 42 CFR 52h, Public Law 103-43) that are strictly enforced. The guidelines for administration of drugs to human subjects can be found at http://www.drugabuse.gov/Funding/HSGuide.html.

[2]   The National Research Council has published the *Guide for the Care and Use of Laboratory Animals*, Eighth Edition (Washington DC: The National Academies Press, 2011), which is strictly enforced at the national level. Any investigator using animals must justify the species and numbers, provide adequate veterinary care, describe provisions for minimizing discomfort and distress, and provide euthanasia if needed.

[3]   For example, two papers that show this are as follows: Ahmed, SH and George Koob. "Long-Lasting Increase in the Set Point for Cocaine Self-Administration after Escalation in Rats." *Psychopharmacology* 146:303-312, 1999. Paterson, NE and A Markou. "Increased Motivation for Self-Administered Cocaine after Escalated Cocaine Intake." *Neuroreport* 14:2229-2232, 2003.

[4]   See endnote 1.

[5]   Lundahl LH and CE Johanson. "Cue-Induced Craving for Marijuana in Cannabis-Dependent Adults." *Exp Clin Psychopharmacol* 19:224-230, 2011.

3

Feeling Good:
The Brain's Own Reward System

What do drugs do for us? An addict was asked why she injects heroin. Her reply was that it is like a dozen orgasms! Although the effects can vary according to the drug, it is safe to say that drugs can make us feel good, or even wonderful. The concepts of pleasure, reward, and reinforcement are so important for drug abuse that we can't leave this topic without describing key discoveries about the brain's own pleasure and reward system. Drugs couldn't produce reward if these capabilities weren't already in the brain.

Prior to experiments showing a drug-related reward described in the previous chapter, there were experiments that revealed a naturally occurring reward and reinforcement system in the brain. Given that the brain works partly by electrical activity, it isn't surprising that these discoveries relied on electrical stimulation of brain regions. If you carry out an action that results in an immediate reward or good feeling, you want to carry out that action again and again, and we all do this every day. The good feelings reinforce (and hence, the idea of "reinforcement") the performance of the actions that produced them. For example, we get to the dining room in time for meals. We learn, develop habits, and so on, in response to rewards. Given that the brain is the organ of behavior, how do we find out where these rewarding and reinforcing actions reside in the brain and what exactly happens in the brain?

To answer these questions, electrodes can be implanted in the brain, stimulated, and the elicited behaviors can be recorded and measured. However, there is also a procedure called electrical *self-stimulation*, which is the process by which rats (and humans) press a lever that delivers an electrical stimulation to some part of the brain. Yes, lever pressing again! Only this time it is not a drug injection but rather a direct electrical stimulation of the brain that is the result. The fact that the animals press the lever again and again means that there is something positive or good about the result of electrical stimulation. But electrical self-stimulation occurs only when the electrodes are in certain parts of the brain, revealing to us the parts of the brain that are involved in giving us rewards or pleasure. This was an important discovery that was made in the 1950s.

Superb Observers and a Big Discovery

Here's how it all started. In 1954, two young scientists, Drs. James Olds and Peter Milner, were trying to find out whether electrical stimulation of a part of the brain called the reticular formation would make rats learn faster. In the course of this work, they noticed that some of the rats that were stimulated for a short time quickly returned to the place in the cage where they experienced the stimulation. The rats returned to the place where they were stimulated again and again, as though they wanted more stimulation! This suggested that there was something positive, rewarding, and reinforcing about stimulating the part of the brain containing the electrodes.

A big surprise was that in the animals behaving this way, the electrodes were not in the reticular formation at all, but rather in another area called the septum. A mistake had been made in calculating where the electrodes should have been placed. Wow! It was an accidental discovery in more ways than one. In subsequent experiments, when the rats were given control over their own stimulation, when they were allowed to press a lever to self-stimulate their brains, they did. This was so striking to Olds and Milner, who realized they were on the verge of a discovery, that they dropped their original planned experiments and decided to study the rewarding and reinforcing properties of the electrical stimulation. They implanted electrodes in various places in the brain to see whether the various brain regions would support lever pressing for electrical stimulation (see Figure 3-1).

James Olds' Own Words

"I applied a brief train of 60 cycle sine-wave electrical current whenever an animal entered one corner of the enclosure. The animal did not stay away from that corner, but rather came back quickly after a brief sortie, which followed the first stimulation and came back even more quickly after a briefer sortie, which followed the second stimulation. By the time the third electrical stimulus had been applied, the animal seemed to be 'coming back for more.'" (Valenstein, E.S., *Brain Stimulation and Motivation*, 1st edition, © 1973. Reprinted by permission of Pearson Education, Inc., Upper Saddle River, NJ.)

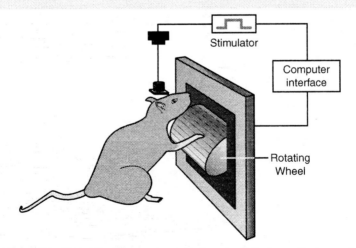

Figure 3-1　This figure depicts a rat rotating a wheel that results in an electrical stimulation of a specific part of the brain. The wheel that rotates produces the same stimulation as a lever that is pressed, and either can be used. The part of the brain that is stimulated is selected by placing an electrode during sterile surgery with anesthesia. In practice, the electrical stimulator is attached to the electrode into the brain by a loose spring so that the animals can move freely about the cage. By systematically exploring brain regions, a map of the "pleasure" centers, for example, sites where animals will self-stimulate, in the brain has been produced. (From Roberts, A.J., and G.F. Koob. "The Neurobiology of Addiction: An Overview." *Alcohol Health & Research World*, 21(2): 101–106, 1997. Updated: October 2000.)

By carefully mapping the sites of the electrodes in the brain[1], they found that there were several regions in the brain that produced this repetitive, reinforcing self-stimulating behavior, and they sometimes referred to these areas as the pleasure center(s). High rates of electrical self-stimulation were found in the lateral hypothalamus, the medial forebrain bundle, and other areas. These anatomical mapping studies have revealed much about the brain regions involved, but for our purposes, we don't need to go into that level of anatomical detail. These regions contain many components that are likely stimulated at the same time, and any one of them can be the contributor to the electrical self-stimulation. Later experiments showed that at least one major component of the medial forebrain bundle supporting electrical self-stimulation was the nerve cells, or neurons, that contain the neurotransmitter dopamine. Electrical self-stimulation of the medial forebrain bundle caused a release of dopamine, and chemicals that blocked dopamine blocked electrical self-stimulation. Drugs like cocaine also cause an increase in dopamine, so drugs and electrical self-stimulation have many of the same effects. Neurotransmitters, including dopamine, and their role in the brain are discussed in more detail in the next chapters.

Works in Humans, Too

Experiments of this type are not done in humans for ethical reasons, unless there is a patient with some severe and debilitating disorder that has not responded to other treatments. Dr. Robert Heath and his colleagues at Tulane in New Orleans put electrodes into the brains of human patients in the 1950s, and they had several important goals. They wanted to cure or ameliorate severe mental illness by direct electrical stimulation of the so-called pleasure centers. At that time, there were few treatment options for such patients.

In an interesting case, one of Heath's patients self-stimulated the septal region of his brain about 1,500 times per hour, showing that this can be a powerful and even consuming effect—this brings to mind the heroin addict quoted in the first paragraph of this chapter. The patient was reminded of and discussed sex during the stimulations. When stimulations were in a different region, the midbrain, the patient had happy thoughts that were not sexual. Other studies resulted in patients describing many different sensations and feelings, such as general pleasure, a sense of well-being, a positive change in mood, pleasant sensations in various body parts, relief from anxiety, and euphoria. What an amazing result!

Overall, the work of Heath and others indicated that there were pleasure or rewarding centers in humans' brains and in animals' brains as shown by Olds and Milner. The notion that the brain is the organ of pleasure as well as pain was here to stay.

Deep Brain Stimulation Today

A useful procedure used today in humans is called deep brain stimulation (DBS), which is not necessarily associated with drugs and pleasure. In this procedure, neurosurgeons implant electrodes into the brains of patients with a battery-powered generator that produces electrical pulses (see Figure 3-2). It has been found that stimulation of the electrodes can relieve symptoms of chronic pain, major depression, Parkinson's disease, and other disorders. Of course, it depends where the electrodes are implanted, and different sites are used for different disorders. This treatment is relatively new because the first use for DBS was approved by the FDA in only 1997. It is interesting that the mechanism of DBS is still not thoroughly understood. It won't surprise you to learn that DBS is being discussed as a treatment for addictive disorders. Promising results have been obtained in animal studies where DBS seems to reduce an animal's interest in self-administering drugs.

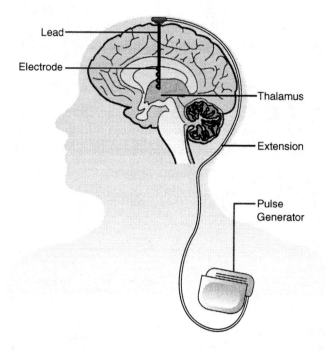

Figure 3-2   Deep brain stimulation is an important therapeutic technique used today that can treat serious neurological disorders. An electrode is placed in the brain region (the thalamus is shown here) that has been found to alleviate certain symptoms. A lead is attached to the electrode and the extension wires are threaded under the skin to a pulse generator that provides the stimulation. The pulse generator is placed under the skin in a region where it can be calibrated and serviced safely. The stimulator is turned on to alleviate various symptoms. (From http://www.medicinenet.com/script/main/art.asp?articlekey=56945, with permission, accessed December 28, 2010.)

Stunning Implications

Following the discovery by Olds and Milner, many thousands of papers have been published on the topic. Electrical stimulation reinforcement, as it came to be called, has been reported in many species examined including not only mammals, but also some fishes and even snails. It is often a robust and powerful effect. In one report, rats pressed levers for stimulation for almost 20 straight days, producing about 29 presses per minute! Self-stimulation has also been connected to food and water intake. At some sites in the brain, the rate of self-stimulation increased with food deprivation and decreased after a meal. Other sites were found to produce varying levels of stimulation as a function of water deprivation. These results supported the idea that there are powerful systems in the brain that reinforce behaviors such as taking food and water. These rewards, as well as those for mating, are critical for our survival as individuals and for survival of the species.[2] It only makes sense that the brain has evolved so as to have a preeminent influence over our survival.

The Drug Connection!

Now for the final piece! We know from the previous chapter that drugs are self-administered, and now we know that certain parts of the brain support electrical self-stimulation. A logical question is this: Are they two completely different entities, or are they connected? In other words, do they access the same thing in our brains? Do the same brain regions mediate both processes?

As it turns out, the two different activities *are* related, and a relatively simple experiment shows this. Rats were allowed to learn to electrically self-stimulate their brains until their lever pressing responses were stable. Then the electrical current was varied until the *threshold* was established. The key to understanding this experiment is to understand thresholds. The threshold is the lowest level of electrical current that will elicit self-stimulation. If less current is used, the rats won't realize that a stimulation has occurred. If the threshold current or more current is used, then the rats recognize it as stimulating. There are established procedures for reliably measuring thresholds.

At this point the self-stimulating rats were injected with varying doses[3] of cocaine, and the thresholds of electrical self-stimulation were determined for each dose of cocaine. It turns out that the threshold for self-stimulation varied according to the dose of cocaine given to the rat. The more cocaine that was given, the lower the threshold became. The threshold was lowered significantly at around the dose of cocaine that caused behavioral effects (see Figure 3-3), and this same result was found when other addicting drugs were used in the experiment.

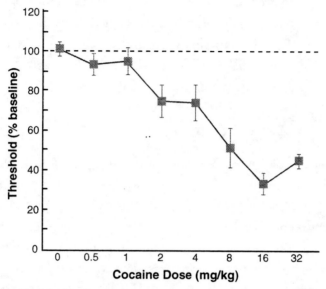

Figure 3-3   Electrical self-stimulation can be studied by varying the amount of electrical current that is passed through the electrode. Obviously, if the current is reduced to a very low level, there will be no self-stimulation because the animal won't recognize it. The threshold is the lowest level of current that will result in self-stimulation (refer to Figure 3-1). An injection of cocaine will lower the threshold! It is as though the drug, by itself, provides some stimulation to the brain region already, and not as much electrical current is needed. Thus, drugs affect the same, endogenous, reward systems that have been identified by electrical self-stimulation. (Reprinted from Elsevier Books, George F. Koob, Michel Le Moal, *Neurobiology of Addiction*, 23-67, Copyright (2006), with permission from Elsevier.)

The interaction between drugs and electrical self-stimulation in specific brain regions shows that they both use the same neuronal pathways in the brain. The drugs raise the activity of the pathways so that less electrical current is needed to reach the threshold for electrical self-stimulation—definitely an informative finding about how drugs are working!

To complete the picture, it was found that there are also sites in the brain related to aversion or avoidance.[4] Drugs of abuse also have aversive properties, and one can guess that the degree of self-administration is influenced by the ratio of rewarding to aversive properties of the drug. In careful experiments, it has been shown that many drugs such as cannabis, cocaine, alcohol, morphine, and others have aversive properties. Many find the taste of alcohol quite bitter and awful, or the smoke from a cigarette overly nauseating and choking. There is likely to be a tolerance, at least for some drugs, to aversive as well as to rewarding effects of drugs. Unfortunately, the rewarding properties of drugs win out too often.

Summary

Among the many parts of the brain, there are several that support electrical self-stimulation. In other words, animals work persistently to get an electrical stimulation of these regions. At least some of these areas are activated by addicting drugs as well. Thus, there are natural, neuronal pathways in the brain that mediate positive feelings and drugs activate some of these same pathways. Drugs act on a brain that is already wired to make us feel good.

Endnotes

[1] A schematic showing the brain regions that support self-stimulation is found in Gardner E.L., "Brain Reward Mechanisms." In Lowinson J.H., Ruiz P, Millman R.B., Langrod J.G. (Eds), *Substance Abuse: A Comprehensive Textbook*, 4th Edition. Philadelphia, PA: Lippincott Williams and Wilkins, pp. 48–97, 2005.

[2] From http://www.hackcanada.com/ice3/wetware/electrical_brain_stimulation.html, accessed December 23, 2010.

[3] The systematic use of varying doses of drugs in scientific experiments is important. In Figure 3-3, the doses of cocaine were varied to show that the threshold depended on the dose. If it was not dependent on dose, then the effect would not be due to the drug, but due to some other stimulus, perhaps simply holding and injecting the animals. To

claim cause and effect, different quantities of the drug must be used to show no effect at low doses and a gradual, graded response as the dose is increased. Dose-response studies are a fundamental tool in studies of drugs.

[4] Spear L.P., Varlinskaya E.I. "Sensitivity to Ethanol and Other Hedonic Stimuli in an Animal Model of Adolescence: Implica-tions for Prevention Science?" *Dev Psychobiol.* Apr;52(3):236-43, 2010. Davis C.M., Riley A.L. "Conditioned Taste Aversion Learning: Implications for Animal Models of Drug Abuse. *Ann N Y Acad Sci.* Feb;1187(2010):247-75. Carlezon W.A. Jr, Thomas M.J. 2009. Biological Substrates of reward and aversion: a nucleus accumbens activity hypothesis. *Neuropharmacology*, 56 Suppl 1:122-132.

4

The ABCs of Drug Action in the Brain

The patient told his counselor that he had fallen into addiction by taking more and more drugs over several months. "I used to be able to stop, but now, if I don't have the stuff, I go crazy. They say it's in my head, my brain. Somehow it's changed..." The patient is right. The brain *is* changed, and to understand that, we need to know how the brain works at the basic level.

The Nerve Cell

Our brain directs our body and its behavior by using its basic functional unit, the nerve cell. The nerve cell, or *neuron*, has a cell body with branching arms called dendrites, a longer thread-like part known as an axon, and nerve terminals that are found at the ends of the axon (see Figure 4-1, left). The nerve terminal typically abuts another neuron that it will influence by releasing a stimulating chemical. The boundary of the cell is the cell membrane, which keeps the neuron intact.

Neurons are arranged sequentially in chains or circuits, but they do not physically connect or touch each other. Rather, they are separated by a tiny space called the synaptic space or synaptic cleft (see Figure 4-1, right). The term "synapse" refers to the junction, including the nerve terminal, the synaptic space, and the cell membrane of the next neuron in the circuit. When a dendrite or nerve cell body is excited electrically, and if the excitation reaches a certain threshold, an electrical impulse known as the "action potential" propagates down the axon. When the action potential reaches the end of the axon and invades the nerve terminals, a different process occurs, which is known as chemical neurotransmission.

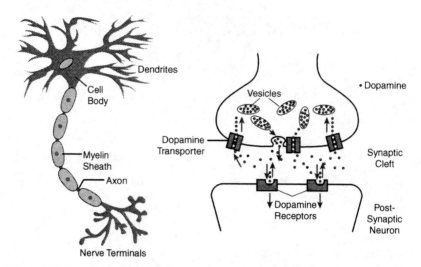

Figure 4-1   Structure and function of the neuron. The schematic on the left shows the structure of a neuron or nerve cell. It has a cell body with dendrites, and an axon that ends in nerve terminals. In this depiction, the axon is covered by a myelin sheath that assists the movement of the action potential (electrical impulse), but the neurons that we discuss do not always have such a sheath. The nerve terminals sit close to the next neuron in the circuit and abut the dendrites on the next cell. This close apposition of nerve terminals and the next neuron (see right side) is fundamental to the way the brain works.

On the right is a schematic of a nerve terminal containing the neurotransmitter dopamine, which abuts the next cell (post synaptic dendrite). Dopamine is stored in the vesicles, and after an action potential (electrical impulse) invades the nerve terminal, the vesicles merge with the membrane to release dopamine into the synaptic cleft or space. The neurotransmitter diffuses across the synapse and then interacts with the receptors and produces a stimulation (indicated by arrows). Finally dopamine is removed from the cleft by the transporter, which moves it back into the nerve terminal where it is stored in the vesicles again. (The left portion is adapted from http://en.wikipedia.org/wiki/Nervous_system. The right portion is reprinted from Trends in Neurosciences, Vol. 14, M.J. Kuhar, M.C. Ritz, and J.W. Boja, "The dopamine hypothesis of the reinforcing properties of cocaine," pp. 299-302, Copyright [1991], with permission from Elsevier.)

Chemical neurotransmission[1] is a chemical signaling process in which a chemical released from the nerve terminal can excite or inhibit the next neuron in the circuit. The chemical is referred to as a neurotransmitter, and there are many different neurotransmitters found in the nervous system. Thus, the brain (or actually individual neurons in a circuit) works by an overall process in which electrical activity in cells and axons alternate with chemical signaling at synapses. The signaling is mediated by receptors, which are described in the following section. This process of chemical neurotransmission is the key, basic process that one needs to understand to know how drugs work in the brain.

The Brain—A Survival Organ

The overall process of neurotransmission works very well and, of course, it should. It has been honed and perfected over eons of evolution. We know that the brain is an organ critical for our survival. The more poorly working versions of the brain (and we assume there were some) were presumably lost because they couldn't compete with "smarter" brains during evolution. When we think of how many different processes are critical for survival, and how the brain mediates and coordinates them, it is truly amazing—even humbling.

Neurotransmitter Synthesis and Storage

The way that neurotransmitters are synthesized depends on which neurotransmitter you are considering. Small molecule neurotransmitters such as dopamine, which is critical for the addiction process (discussed later), are made from amino acid precursors through the actions of enzymes. An enzyme is nothing more than a protein that makes new molecules by facilitating molecular changes. The changes that are made can result in building structures by adding atoms or joining smaller molecules together. Conversely the changes can be a *breakdown* of molecules by removing atoms or by splitting off parts of molecules. Several enzymes often act in a sequence to produce neurotransmitter molecules, which are unique structures. The substances produced and altered along the way are referred to as intermediates. For example, dopamine is made from a widely occurring amino acid, tyrosine. An OH (hydroxyl, oxygen, and hydrogen bound together) group is added to the tyrosine by the enzyme tyrosine hydroxylase to produce the intermediate dihydroxyphenylalanine (DOPA). Then that intermediate is acted upon by the enzyme DOPA decarboxylase to produce dopamine. Because each neurotransmitter has a unique structure, it is synthesized by its own unique set of enzymes and processes. The enzymes and processes needed for the production of neurotransmitters usually are found in the cell body of the neuron, which is where neurotransmitters are produced.

Neurotransmitters are powerful and even dangerous in that they can profoundly alter neuronal function through their signaling properties, especially if they interact with receptors in the wrong place and at the wrong time. Since such stray neurotransmitters could create signaling confusion, the neurons use storage vesicles which are small, membrane-bound containers capable of sequestering large amounts of neurotransmitters. Neurotransmitters are synthesized usually in the cell body and shipped in storage vesicles to the nerve terminals for action-potential-regulated release of neurotransmitters into the synapse.

Many Different Neurotransmitters

There is a surprising variety of neurotransmitters. They can be small molecules such as dopamine, or, they can be mega-molecules such as endorphin, which are equivalent to multiples of molecules the size of dopamine. They can even be gases such as nitric oxide (NO). Some neurotransmitters are excitatory (they excite the next neuron in the circuit) such as glutamate, and others are inhibitory such as gamma-aminobutyric acid (GABA). Having both excitatory and inhibitory signals enables greater control over neuronal activity.

Although it is not surprising that there is more than one neurotransmitter, it appears that there are dozens of neurotransmitters, which is somewhat of a surprise. Scientists speculate that neurotransmitters, in general, are so important for brain function that evolution has provided us with many. They might provide a *margin of safety* so that if a genetic mutation deletes one neurotransmitter, we are not totally impaired.

If our goal is to understand how different drugs of abuse work in the brain, we need to know about neurotransmitters because each drug of abuse can be linked to altering the actions of specific neurotransmitters (see Table 4-1).

TABLE 4-1   Drugs of Abuse and Related Neurotransmitters

Drug	Neurotransmitter
Nicotine	Acetylcholine
Alcohol	Gamma-aminobutyric acid (GABA) and glutamate
Psychostimulants (cocaine and amphetamines)	Dopamine
Opiates	Enkephalins and endorphins
Antianxiety drugs (Xanax and valium)	Gamma-aminobutyric acid (GABA)
Inhalants	Gamma-aminobutyric acid (GABA)
Hallucinogens (LSD)	Serotonin
Caffeine	Adenosine
Marijuana	Endocannabinoids and anadamide
PCP	Glutamate

Drugs that are abused and cause addiction interfere with the action of some neurotransmitter. Each drug in a particular class affects the same neurotransmitter. Occasionally, a single drug can affect more than one neurotransmitter.

Receptors—How Neurotransmitters Work

The gold at the end of the neurotransmission rainbow is the receptor, which is a protein that is selective for a given neurotransmitter just as a given key is selective for a certain lock. A receptor for dopamine will not bind to the neurotransmitter glutamate or any other neurotransmitter for that matter. When a neurotransmitter is released, it diffuses across the synaptic cleft (see Figure 4-1, right) and binds to its receptor. When the neurotransmitter binds, and this is the important part, it changes the shape of the receptor so that the receptor produces some change in the neuron. So the receptor (along with the neurotransmitter, of course) is the element that induces and mediates the change in the next neuron in the circuit. It is also important to know that the neurotransmitters bind to the receptors *reversibly* so that after they act at the receptor and induce a postsynaptic change, they then move away from the receptor. The significance of this is discussed later in this chapter.

There are several different kinds of receptors categorized by the way they work or their structure. Two major kinds are the ion channel receptors and the G-protein coupled receptors. Ion channel receptors were named because when the neurotransmitter binds, it opens an ion channel, which is part of the receptor, and ions flow through it and thereby change the electrical charge in the neuron (see Figure 4-2). Ion channel receptors work quickly (in milliseconds) and are responsible, for example, for the contraction of muscles and movements.

The other major class of receptors is the G-protein coupled receptors (GPCRs). They are so named because they involve G-proteins in their signaling. The overall process is somewhat slow, occurring over seconds sometimes. When the neurotransmitter binds, the subsequent shape change in the receptor allows the G-protein—which is inside the cell and reversibly attached to the receptor—to become activated; then the activated G-protein diffuses in the nerve cell body and induces many different functions. Just as there are many different neurotransmitters, there are also many different G-proteins. This provides neurons with a marvelous variety of ways to produce needed changes. This variety is even greater because an individual neurotransmitter such as dopamine can have many subtypes of receptors that use different kinds of intracellular signaling!

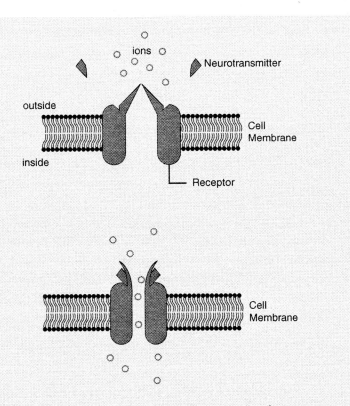

Figure 4-2 Neurotransmitter receptors mediate signaling from one neuron to the next.

This figure shows one of the major kinds of receptors in the brain, the lig-and-gated ion channel receptor, which does exactly as its name implies. When the neurotransmitter that is released from the previous neuron binds to the receptor, a gate opens and the channel in the receptor allows the passage of ions that change the electrical charge and voltage across the membrane. This in turn can cause an action potential (electrical impulse) in the postsynaptic cell. This is one example of how a neurotransmitter released from one neuron can change the properties of the next neuron through a receptor. (Adapted from http://en.wikipedia.org/wiki/File:Three_conformation_states_of_acetylcholine_receptor.jpg.)

In any case, the important thing for those of us focusing on drug abuse is that there are many kinds of signaling and receptors in the brain. They are complex and varied, and, you can say, offer many opportunities for abused drugs to influence the brain. Knowing all of the different kinds of receptors is not critical for knowing how drugs act, but knowing about receptors in general is important.

Removing Neurotransmitters—Making the Message Discreet

Neurotransmitters bind to their receptors in a reversible fashion—they go on and come off. Because the concentration of neurotransmitters is so high in the synaptic space immediately after release, the receptors get stimulated even though the neurotransmitters don't stay on the receptors forever. After the neurotransmitters are bound to the receptors, signals occur, but—and this is significant—the signals *must be terminated* by removal of the neurotransmitters from the receptors and the synapse. If neurotransmission is not terminated, its action is not discrete, and might simply appear to be noise. The ways that the neurotransmitters can be removed from the receptor include the breakdown of the neurotransmitter into inactive products, removal from the synapse by reuptake for recycling, or by diffusion away from the receptors out of the synaptic space. Neurotransmitter breakdown requires enzymes, and reuptake requires a transporter, which is a protein in the nerve terminal membrane that transports the neurotransmitter back into the nerve terminal where it is again stored in vesicles. It is released again by the next action potential.

When we think of a neurotransmitter that is inactivated by being broken down, we often think of acetylcholine, historically the first substance believed to be a neurotransmitter. Like other neurotransmitters, it has several subtypes of receptors in different parts of the body, but its mechanism of termination is always the same. Acetylcholine is broken down by the enzyme acetylcholinesterase (see Figure 4-3) into inactive pieces.

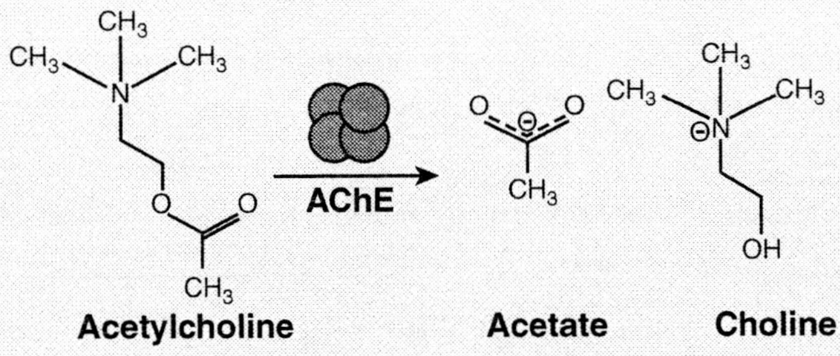

Figure 4-3   Enzymatic breakdown of acetylcholine.

The molecular structure of the neurotransmitter acetylcholine is shown. A globular model of the enzyme, acetylcholinesterase (AChE) is shown breaking down acetylcholine into two smaller molecules, acetate and choline. Neither acetate nor choline are active at receptors so neurotransmission is effectively terminated by AChE, which is present in the synaptic cleft. (Image adapted from www.proteopedia.org/.../Acetylcholinesterase, accessed March 14, 2009.)

Another kind of neurotransmitter is called a peptide, which is often very large. Peptides are broken down by a specific set of enzymes called peptidases. They basically chop up the peptide neurotransmitters into smaller pieces so that they aren't functional any more.

Reuptake is a process of termination that has been linked to many neurotransmitters. For example, dopamine, a neurotransmitter connected to drug abuse and addiction, is removed from the synapse by reuptake via a transporter appropriately called the dopamine transporter (DAT) (see Figure 4-1, right). The transporter is like a pump that moves the neurotransmitter from outside the nerve terminal back inside. This removes the neurotransmitter from the receptors and effectively stops its action. Psychostimulant drugs, such as cocaine, amphetamine, and methamphetamine, are well known to block this transporter, resulting in an excess of dopamine in the synapse.

The Overall Process of Chemical Signaling

We need to keep in mind that the normal brain requires the three Rs—release of neurotransmitter, receptor activation by neurotransmitter, and removal of neurotransmitter. When any of these are disturbed, you can get toxicity or disease of some kind. Despite this, it is important to remember that helpful therapeutic drugs and medications also target these processes with much benefit. For example, certain antidepressants block the reuptake of serotonin, thereby prolonging the action of serotonin in the synapse.

Abused Drugs Distort Neurotransmission

Now we can begin to put all of this together and consider how drugs of abuse affect the brain. Abused drugs can distort the functions of neurotransmitters by mimicking or blocking neurotransmitters in *uncontrolled* ways. This distorts our behaviors that are regulated by the brain and alters our sensations. *Uncontrolled* means that the brain itself doesn't have any mechanism to regulate them.

Because abused drugs in the brain are chemical signals, they are similar to neurotransmitters. But they are different from neurotransmitters in important ways. Neurotransmitters and the brain have co-evolved over eons of time, and they coexist quite peacefully. Neurotransmitters are beautifully regulated by the brain. When their levels are low, they are synthesized. When made, they are safely stored in vesicles. When needed, they are released from specific neurons. After they are released and stimulate receptors, their action is terminated by breakdown, diffusion, or reuptake. Drugs of abuse, on the other hand, get into the brain and affect neurotransmission, but the brain does not have ways to handle or terminate their actions! Drug levels in the brain are under the control of the drug taker and not regulated by synthetic enzymes or release or reuptake in the brain. Drugs are not easily removed from receptors like neurotransmitters, and therefore the actions of drugs persist in time far longer than those of neurotransmitters. Drug-induced signals can be greater than those produced by neurotransmitters and last longer as well. Thus, it is not surprising that drugs can overpower the brain. They are much like a Trojan Horse. They enter the brain by natural processes, but when in the brain they create havoc!

Cocaine's Actions—An Example

Dopamine-containing neurons (or dopaminergic neurons) are critical for addiction to occur, particularly to psychostimulant drugs such as cocaine.[2] Many different drugs, although they might act at many different sites and produce many different effects, share the same effect in that they cause a release of dopamine. When dopaminergic neurons are activated and an action potential develops, the electrical impulse moves down the axon into the nerve terminal, and dopamine is released from the nerve terminal. It then diffuses across the synaptic cleft and stimulates dopamine receptors. The action at receptors is terminated by removing dopamine from the cleft by the dopamine transporter, which then transports dopamine from the synaptic space back into the nerve terminal. That is the normal progression of events.

Now enter cocaine! Cocaine blocks the dopamine transporter and the uptake of dopamine.[3] Because it blocks the removal of dopamine, dopamine levels in the synapse rise sharply, thereby prolonging and enhancing the process of dopamine-mediated neurotransmission. The brain itself does not have a mechanism to shut down cocaine's actions. It can't be removed by uptake or broken down in the brain, although drugs are removed from the brain and blood by metabolic breakdown in the liver. However, this process in the liver is very slow (sometimes hours) compared to the time of neurotransmission, which is a fraction of a second. So the intense and prolonged stimulation of dopamine receptors continues for as long as the drug user uses the drug. This level of stimulation probably rarely, if ever, occurs under normal circumstances. Somehow, this prolongation and intensification of dopamine receptor stimulation is key for the addictive process (see Figures 4-4 and 4-5). Excess dopamine has been associated with increased reward or motivation.

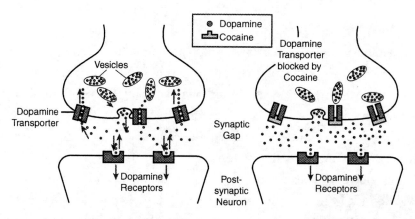

Figure 4-4   The dopamine nerve terminal and cocaine.

This diagram (partly repeated from Figure 4-1) shows the three steps of neurotransmission on the left: (1) release of dopamine from vesicles into the synaptic cleft, (2) interaction with receptors, and then (3) removal of dopamine from the synapse by reuptake. On the right side of the diagram, note that cocaine disrupts this three-step process and blocks the reuptake by blocking the dopamine transporter. This causes dopamine levels to increase at the receptors and to increase signaling. The brain can't control this problem, because it does not have a way to remove cocaine. (Reprinted from *Trends in Neurosciences*, Vol. 14, M.J. Kuhar, M.C. Ritz, and J.W. Boja, "The dopamine hypothesis of the reinforcing properties of cocaine," pp. 299-302, Copyright [1991], with permission from Elsevier.)

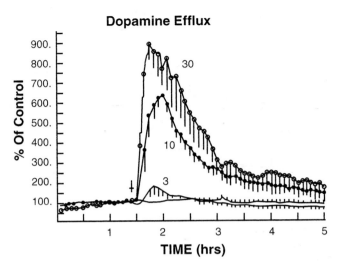

Dopamine Efflux

Figure 4-5   Cocaine blocks the dopamine transporter and extracellular levels of dopamine in the brain increase sharply. The horizontal-axis shows the time after a cocaine injection, which was given at about 1½ hours (vertical arrow). The vertical axis shows the levels of dopamine in the brain region called the striatum relative to the time before the cocaine injection. The highest curve shows dopamine levels after an injection of 30 mg/kg of cocaine, the next lower curve after an injection of 10 mg/kg, and the next lower curve after an injection of 3 mg/kg. The lowest curve shows dopamine levels after no injection and is a continuation of the baseline. Dopamine levels rose about ninefold (to 900 percent of control) after an injection of 30 mg/kg. This is an experimental confirmation of the idea shown in Figure 4-4. This figure shows data from one of the first experiments of this type and was produced by Dr. Jay Justice and his colleagues. (Reprinted from *European Journal of Pharmacology*, Vol. 139, W.H. Church, J.B. Justice Jr., and L.D. Byrd, "Extracellular dopamine in rat striatum following uptake inhibition by cocaine, nomifensine and benztropine," pp. 345-348, Copyright [1987], with permission from Elsevier.)

Another drug that disrupts normal neurotransmission is morphine, which is an opioid or opiate drug. Morphine stimulates receptors in the brain for the neurotransmitters enkephalins and endorphins. Morphine does not do anything to the uptake, diffusion, or metabolism of a neurotransmitter. Rather, it stimulates receptors. Actually, most drugs work by doing something to receptors, either stimulating them or inhibiting them. When the drug user injects or takes morphine orally, it goes from the blood to the brain where it stimulates the receptors that are there for endorphins and enkephalin. However, the brain does not have a way to remove or stop the action of morphine like it does for enkephalin and endorphin (which is by diffusion and breakdown by peptidases). Morphine is metabolized in the body, but the process is slow compared to the time for a natural neurotransmission event, so the time course of neuro-transmission is greatly distorted by the drug! Again, neurotransmission at opioid synapses is greatly enhanced and prolonged by morphine (and other opiate drugs) to a degree that might never occur naturally. Morphine taken by the user commandeers opioid neuro-transmission in the brain. Because it makes the user feel good, he or she will control the levels of drug in the brain according to how he or she feels and how much drug is available. It is interesting that mor-phine, through some neuronal circuit, also increases dopamine levels.

So what does all this mean? One interesting implication is that the abuse of drugs and addiction has a physiological basis in the brain. It involves a significant change in neurotransmitter function in spe-cific brain regions. Because drug abuse and addiction have a physio-logical bases, rather than a mystical or spiritual one, it is unlikely that these disorders are due to a fatal flaw in moral character or a lack of self-control. This is important to emphasize because therapeutic medications generally target physiologic processes also. Therefore, medications can be developed for drug users, and, in fact, many help-ful medications to combat drug abuse are currently in use.

Speed of Drug Entry into Brain: Fast Is Best!

The speed at which drugs enter the brain seems critically important. When drugs enter the blood stream, they reach the brain by the reg-ular circulation of blood. However, just reaching the brain is not the only factor in producing actions in the brain. The rate or speed of drug entry into the brain has been shown to be important.

When a drug is taken by mouth, it gets into the stomach and then is absorbed into the blood. This route is a slow route for drugs compared to other methods of drug delivery. Direct injection of drug into blood (intravenously) can produce quick effects, much faster than by the oral route. Snorting drugs into the lungs or smoking are also fast because the absorption of drugs from lung to blood is quick as well. This is relevant because drugs that enter the brain faster produce a greater or more intense *rush* than drugs entering more slowly. Methods that produce a greater rush and high have a greater addiction liability. This has been shown in both animal[4] and human studies and seems well established. One study[5] showed that smoking 50 mg of cocaine produced a high in less than 1 minute, but taking 96 mg intranasally didn't produce an equivalent high even after 5 minutes. Understanding this helps us understand the overall process of addiction and suggests also that potential medicines for drug users, particularly those medicines with some drug-like properties, might be best if they enter the brain slowly to avoid being highly addicting themselves!

Why is the rate of entry of a drug into the brain important? Again, we think it is because of the way the brain is constructed, functions and has evolved. Our senses, which include, for example, hearing, smelling, and seeing, are obviously critical for survival. But it is not only the simple *detection* of sounds, odors, and objects that are critical, but also the *rate of change* in these sensations that contributes to our survival.[6] When a sound suddenly changes in volume, or when an object moves, it becomes more noticeable. In other words, *changes* in our environment are more readily detected in our awareness! We all have been at loud parties where we adapt to the music and racket. But, if there is a sudden change in a particular sound, such as a new record being played, or a loud announcement, we hear it and attend to it. If we are looking at a landscape, we might not notice an animal or person in the scene until it moves, and we know that lying still can help us evade detection. So, our senses are geared to detect changes in environment more readily than slow or unchanging scenes. You can easily imagine that this has survival advantage because sudden threats or treats will be picked up and acted on. Changes in sensations are more readily detected, and faster changes are detected faster!

This applies to drug taking because drugs that enter the brain more quickly produce greater changes in our sensations than drugs that enter more slowly. In other words, a greater rush is produced when drugs enter the brain faster or at a greater rate, and getting a rush or high is often the reason for taking drugs. Drugs can enter the brain and be detected faster for at least two reasons. One is that, because of the chemical structure and solubility of some substances, they can more easily penetrate into the brain. The second is that humans can control the rate at which they take the drug. Smoking crack cocaine gets cocaine into the brain faster than swallowing it. Injecting a drug into the blood stream gets the drug into the brain faster than swallowing or snorting it. Therefore, smokable or injectable forms of drugs have a greater danger of producing abuse or addiction.

The way the brain functions and has evolved plays an important role in how drug users select drugs and the methods they use to administer the drugs. This explains why the brain loses control over drug-influenced chemical signaling and how the brain has a natural vulnerability to addiction.

Plasticity—A Biggie!

Another thing to remember about signaling in the brain is that circuits and signaling pathways are not static. Levels of neurotransmitters, receptors, transporters, and other proteins can change in response to various stimuli! In other words, the brain has flexibility in its structure, biochemistry, and responses. This flexibility, or the ability of the brain to change in response to stimuli, is called *plasticity*, which is seriously important. It underlies learning and adaptations to changes in environment, and it can be caused in many ways including repeatedly taking a drug. Plasticity underlies addiction, and a key goal of research into drug addiction focuses on discovering and understanding the nature of these plasticities. Plasticity in response to drugs is described further in Chapter 5, "The Dark Side Develops!"

Summary

This chapter describes the basic brain machinery for chemical neurotransmission and how drugs interfere in that process. Directly or indirectly, drugs can do the same thing that neurotransmitters do, such as stimulate receptors, or they can block functions, such as cocaine blocking the transporter for dopamine. When drugs are in the brain, the brain cannot control the drugs like it can control neurotransmitters. Drug action in the brain is more under the control of the drug user. This is a significant part of why drugs basically can *take over* the brain. In the next chapter, we see that drugs, because of this aberrant behavior, can produce significant effects in the brain.

Endnotes

[1] The discovery of chemical neurotransmission is an interesting story. A major part of the discovery is due to Otto Loewi, a German Jewish scientist and refugee working at NYU. He carried out a definitive experiment in 1921 that has become famous, along with the anecdote of how it happened. It was known that if you stimulated the vagus nerve leading to the heart, the heart's beating slowed. But Loewi extended this and took some of the fluid from the slowing heart and applied it to another heart, and found that it also slowed! He correctly proposed that a chemical substance was released from the stimulated vagus nerve onto the heart muscle, which resulted in a slowing of the beating of the heart. This substance in fact turned out to be acetylcholine, the first accepted neurotransmitter. An interesting part of this story is that the idea for the experiment came to him in his sleep one night, and in his dreamy state he wrote it down on a scrap of paper on his nightstand. In the morning, much to his horror, he

couldn't read his writing, nor could he remember the dream! Luckily, the next night he had the same dream, and this time he got out of bed and immediately went to the laboratory and did this definitive experiment. Thirteen years later, he was awarded the Nobel Prize for his "dream experiment!"

2   The following is a brief summary of the history of the dopamine story and drug addiction. It is a personal communication from Dr. Roy Wise, a longtime, productive researcher in this field.

The earliest work was by Olds (a) who showed that nonselective drugs like chlorpromazine and reserpine (whose effects included a blunting of dopamine's effects) antagonized electrical brain stimulation reward. Stein generated a theory of reward that proposed that norepinephrine was the key neurotransmitter, but this was not supported by subsequent data (b, c). When selective dopamine antagonists became available, they, and selective destruction of dopamine-containing neurons showed effects on reward. This implicated dopamine and not norepinephrine or other neurotransmitters in brain stimulation reward (d, e). Pickens and Harris were the first to suggest that the substrates of brain stimulation reward and psychostimulant reward were perhaps the same (f).

Yokel and I (g) and Davis and Smith (h) were the first to show that amphetamine lost its rewarding action if the dopamine system was selectively blocked, and de Wit and I (i) and Risner and Jones (j) showed the same result with cocaine. Roberts showed that selective dopamine (but not norepinephrine) lesions disrupted cocaine reward (k). These were the first studies to show that dopamine function was necessary for cocaine and amphetamine reward. Yokel and I then showed that a dopamine agonist, apomorphine, (a compound that directly stimulated dopamine receptors) was self-administered (g, l), which confirmed that dopamine activation was also sufficient for drug-related reward. Ritz et al., (m) took the story further by showing that the initial site of action of cocaine and the psychostimulants— specifically for their rewarding and reinforcing actions—was the dopamine transporter rather than some other site. Initial work in knockout mice suggested that cocaine might still be rewarding in animals lacking the dopamine transporter (n), but more recent work questions this finding and shows, rather, the opposite (o).

(a) J. Olds, K. F. Killam, P. Bach y Rita, *Science*, 124, 265 (1956). (b) L. Stein, *J Psychiat Res* 8, 345 (1971). (c) S. K. Roll, *Science*, 168, 1370 (1970). (d) A. S. Lippa, S. M. Antelman, A. E. Fisher, D. R. Canfield, *Pharmacology Biochemistry and Behavior*, 1, 23 (1973). (e) G. Fouriezos, R. A. Wise, *Brain Research*, 103, 377 (1976). (f) R. Pickens, W. C. Harris, *Psychopharmacologia* 12, 158 (1968). (g) R. A. Yokel, R. A. Wise, *Science* 187, 547 (1975). (h) W. M. Davis, S. G. Smith, *Journal of Pharmacy and Pharmacology*, 27, 540 (1975). (i) H. de Wit, R. A. Wise, *Can J Psychol*, 31, 195 (1977). (j) M. E. Risner, B. E. Jones, *Psychopharmacology*, 71, 83 (1980). (k) D. C. S. Roberts, M. E. Corcoran, H. C. Fibiger, *Pharmacology Biochemistry and Behavior*, 6, 615 (1977). (l) R. A. Yokel, R. A. Wise, *Psychopharmacology (Berl)*, 58, 289 (1978). (m) M.C. Ritz et al., 1987. Science 237: 1219–1223. (n) B. A. Rocha et al., *Nature Neuroscience*, 1, 132 (1998). (o) M. Thomsen, D. D. Han, H. H. Gu, S. B. Caine, *J Pharmacol Exp*, Ther 331, 204 (2009).

[3] The dopamine transporter (DAT) is known as the initial site of action of cocaine that produces the addicting properties of the drug. This was shown more or less definitely in a paper in 1987 using "receptor binding," a technique that reveals the initial site of action of drugs. The problem before that was that cocaine has many actions. It not only inhibits the uptake of dopamine, but it also inhibits the uptake of serotonin and norepinephrine, two additional neurotransmitters. Moreover, cocaine produces a local analgesia by blocking sodium channels in nerves, and it has other actions, too. So, which is the site that makes cocaine an abused drug? A team at the National Institute on Drug Abuse, lead by Drs. Mike Kuhar and Mary Ritz, compared the capability of cocaine and several cocaine analogs to inhibit the uptake of neurotransmitters with the capability of these chemicals to be self-administered (SA) by animals. The drugs that were potent at the DAT were the ones potent in drug SA, and the drugs weak at DAT were the ones weak in SA. This correlation was strong and statistically valid. There was other existing evidence for this at the time, but this binding experiment solidly confirmed the idea. The reference is Ritz M et. al. "Cocaine Receptors on Dopamine Transporters Are Related to the Self-Administration of Cocaine." *Science*, 237: 1219–1223, (1987).

4   An example of a study with animals showing that compounds with
    a faster onset of action were better reinforcers is Kimmel H et al.
    Pharmacol Biochem Behav, 86:45–54, 2007. An example of a study
    with human subjects showing that the rate of entry of cocaine into
    the brain determines its reinforcing (addicting) effects, as
    described in the text is Volkow N.D. et al. *Life Sciences*,
    67:1507–1515, 2000.

5   Ibid.

6   This idea derives from studies of the sensory systems in our bod-
    ies. Many highly technical experiments on vision and touch show
    that individual neurons in the periphery and brain respond to
    changes, either increases or decreases, in stimuli. For example,
    this can be seen in the responses of ganglion cells in the retina, in
    cortical neurons responding to mechanoreceptors, and in rapidly
    adapting mechanoreceptors in skin. Details of these studies can be
    found in a textbook such as Kandel et al., *Principles of Neural
    Science*, Third edition (Appleton and Lange, 1991). While the
    rush derived from drugs has not yet been subjected to such care-
    ful scrutiny, it seems reasonable to propose that a drug-induced
    high or rush is due to *changes* in the basic sensations.

5 —————————————

The Dark Side Develops!

Tim, an Iraq veteran who lost both legs in a roadside ambush where most of his buddies died, has been taking drugs for years. He's been diagnosed with Post-traumatic Stress Disorder (PTSD) and uses several drugs, including alcohol, to help him relax and sleep. He is distressed that he has gradually needed more and more drugs to get to sleep, even for a short time. This has added to his troubles because of the increasing cost, and searching for drugs seems to dominate his activities. He is beginning to worry that he is addicted.

Drugs literally dominate the brain because the brain doesn't have an adequate defense against drugs. But there is more to addiction than that. If a drug is taken once, it distorts the way the brain functions, but is that addiction? No, the development of addiction almost always requires repeated drug taking. That is not to say that a single drug experience cannot be profound. Indeed, drug users have said things such as, "The first time I took heroin I knew it was special for me. With heroin, I could do anything or get through anything." In fact, sometimes drug users try to re-experience that first, special high or feeling. They are chasing something they might or might not fully experience again. But, they keep trying—with disastrous effects.

A compelling account of the disaster of addiction is given in the book, *Methland,* (Bloomsbury, USA), by Nick Reding. He describes how a highly addictive substance like methamphetamine, called crank or crystal meth, literally took over the economy and social fabric of various, poor Midwestern towns. In some cases, the drug was given away for people to try, and they returned with a vengeance to buy it. There were the expected stories of users messing up their health, relationships, and jobs. Some turned to making or "cooking" methamphetamine themselves, maybe to save money or to make money by dealing the drug. Unfortunately, it is a dangerous process where the containers can explode. Many injured addicts, people with severe scars from burns or missing fingers from explosions, still learned to hold, light, and smoke a pipe to get the drug. Drug dependence can be unbelievably gripping.

The drive to take drugs is a curious thing. Sometimes it is more of a drive just to take a drug than it is to get high. Drug abusers say that drugs produce euphoria, but for most people, that doesn't last! Cocaine doesn't always get them high anymore but they still can't stop.[1] Initially the high can be better than anything, but after several months, the euphoria can be gone and you are still driven to get drugs even though it is disrupting your life. The state of addiction can be more of a compulsion or a motivation than actually getting high. As the simple choice to take a drug the first time becomes compulsive drug use, many things are happening in the brain.

George Koob, a neuropsychopharmacologist, studies changes in the brain due to drugs and he refers to them as the "dark side" of addiction. He notes that with continued drug taking, deficits develop in the reward system, and brain stress systems become sensitized. This suggests that with more drug use, there is less reward or feeling good, and a greater response to stress. Moreover, he has specified the neuronal pathways and neurotransmitters involved in these processes, which will foster much future research. His work is explored and extended by many researchers.

Demons in the Brain—Addiction and Withdrawal

The addicted brain is like having a drug-craving demon in your brain. But as repeated drug use creates the addicted brain, there is another important demon in the brain called *withdrawal*. Withdrawal occurs when an individual stops taking drugs and then develops symptoms that are often the opposite of the feelings that the drug produces. For example, an effect of cocaine is mental stimulation, and a symptom of withdrawal from cocaine is depression. Besides making the addict feel terrible, withdrawal is an impetus to relapse to drug use because taking more drugs relieves withdrawal. Fear of withdrawal is also likely to be an impediment to getting treatment. So, withdrawal is a big part of the complex picture that we have been examining. But how does it happen, and how do we think of it?

A relatively simple way to think of addiction and withdrawal is to look at a seesaw (see Figure 5-1). Consider that someone is functioning normally and doesn't have anything to do with drugs. This normal state can be represented by the seesaw that is level or in balance and not touching the ground on either side. But when drugs are taken repeatedly, the brain is battered by changes in chemical signaling and is driven to a new state, one represented by the seesaw pushed down (by the drug) on one side—the brain can change and is capable of plasticity.[2] As drugs push the seesaw down, the brain compensates by pushing in the opposite direction to get the seesaw level and in balance. Taking enough drugs over a long enough period of time results in an accumulation of compensatory changes in the brain, which is addiction. If drug taking stops, the brain's counterbalancing efforts are unopposed and the seesaw is either pushed up or down on the opposite side. This is where the drug taker can experience unpleasant feelings or physiological symptoms of withdrawal. For some drugs such as alcohol, withdrawal can be medically serious and even life threatening. Withdrawal interferes with everyday tasks and can drive the drug user to do many things, even dangerous and destructive crimes to get more drugs. But, if he or she succeeds in staying away from drugs for a long enough time, the brain readjusts, and the fictional seesaw eventually shifts back so that it is level and balanced, and the original, normal state is regained—at least theoretically. Realistically though, staying away from drugs is not easy to do once you are hooked.

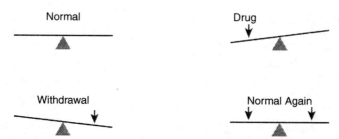

Figure 5-1   Drugs change the normal balance in the brain. The balanced see-saw represents brain neurochemistry in a drug-free state (for example, before the brain has been exposed to drugs). Consuming drugs unbalances brain chemistry to produce the effects associated with drug use. The drug symbolically pushes the seesaw down and the brain pushes in the opposite direction in an effort to restore balance. If the drug is removed, the unbalance is exposed, and the brain's neurochemistry is driven in the opposite direction (withdrawal). Removing the drug results in a withdrawal syndrome that includes signs and symptoms that are often opposite to the drug's effects. Withdrawal continues until the adaptation can be reduced resulting a normal state again. (Adapted from John Littleton, *Alcohol Health & Research World*, Vol 22, 13–24, 1998.)

However we think of it, we know that repeated drug taking changes the brain and that stopping drug use results in an unpleasant state of withdrawal. Symptoms of withdrawal by drug-dependent subjects can be dramatic, but they vary according to the drug that is used. Withdrawal symptoms for alcohol, for example, include irritability, agitation, craving for more alcohol, insomnia, sweating, diarrhea, rapid heartbeat, increased blood pressure, and even seizures. On the other hand, withdrawal from caffeine, which is only a mild stimulant, produces fatigue, sedation, and headaches. For some drugs, hallucinations can be prominent. One methamphetamine addict in jail was convinced that one of the veins in his arm was a strip of metal, and he spent hours using his fingernails trying to dig it out. These dramatic distortions in physiology and behavior demonstrate the power of drugs in the brain.

Gotta Have More and More

One of the hallmarks of addiction is *tolerance* to the addicted substance. It means that more and more drugs are needed over time to produce the same response, or that the same dose of drugs now produces a lesser response. If you originally got high on one pill of a drug, with continued use it might take three times as much drug to get a similar high. So addiction is not only the compulsion to keep taking the drug, but also, in many cases, the compulsion to take more and more drugs to get the same response. A basis of tolerance is at least partly due to changes in the molecules of synaptic transmission. Tolerance is well documented in humans for many drugs. For some drugs, at least part of tolerance is due to the fact that the liver adapts and metabolizes the drug faster. However, many changes in the brain are also needed to explain tolerance. Dr. Bill Dewey, Professor at Virginia Commonwealth University, along with others, have described how tolerance has many different mechanisms in different tissues. It is more appropriate to talk about many different kinds of tolerances, rather than just one tolerance.

With psychostimulants such as cocaine or amphetamine, a reverse tolerance or *sensitization* can occur. The same dose of drug now produces a greater response instead of a lesser response, and this has been studied in animals. Both tolerance and sensitization are regarded as adaptations of the brain[3] to repeated drug taking.

What Is Happening in the Brain?

The brain is the organ of behavior, and if we have a compulsive drug-taking habit, then that compulsivity is based in the brain. We know from the previous chapter that drugs of abuse change chemical signaling, and this chapter explores how chemical signaling can change gene and protein expression. Because we have directly measured gene expression in the brain, we know that drugs do in fact produce such changes.

Every cell in our body, including neurons in the brain, has a nucleus that contains chromosomes. Each chromosome has a number of genes, which are made up of stretches of deoxyribonucleic acid (DNA) (see Figures 5-2 and 5-3), and genes are units that code for a particular protein. Proteins in the body produce obvious traits such as hair color or the particular sound of our voice.

DNA ⟶ mRNA ⟶ Protein

Figure 5-2   The DNA in our genes code for specific proteins. This simple figure is one of the most important. It shows that DNA, which is the material that contains our genes in the chromosomes, is the template on which messenger ribonucleic acid (mRNA) is made. In turn, mRNA is the template on which proteins are made. A mutation in our genes, which is a change in the structure of our DNA (see Figure 5-3), leads to a changed protein, which might or might not be functional. The proteins in our body are ultimately responsible for how we look and behave. Something that is not shown schematically is how the activity of the gene is regulated. Special proteins, called transcription factors, bind to the DNA and regulate the levels of mRNA and protein that are produced. Neurotransmitters can regulate the activity of transcription factors. Thus, drugs can alter gene expression and ultimately protein levels.

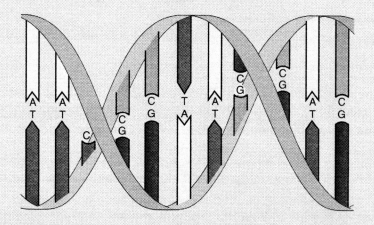

Figure 5-3   The helical structure of DNA. The DNA molecule is composed of two similar and complementary strands that bind together. The strands are like a twisted ladder (helix), where the rungs are the special chemicals or bases that make up the genetic code. The names of the bases are abbreviated as A, T, C, and G. A gene is a length of DNA that ultimately produces a protein. By complementary, we mean that Gs and Cs always match up and As and Ts always match up. Each group of three bases make up a codon that codes for a specific amino acid. So, all of the proteins in our body are specified by the codons in our genes. A mutation occurs when one of the bases is changed, for example, a G to a C. This changes the protein that is made by one amino acid, but that can be significant in some cases. (Adapted from: http://en.wikipedia.org/wiki/File:Dna-SNP.svg, accessed January 24, 2011.)

But the effect of most genes and their proteins are more subtle and do not produce an obvious or visible trait. Rather the proteins might help the brain function in several different ways: by facilitating chemical neurotransmission in certain parts of the brain, by changing the number of synapses in certain places, or by changing energy metabolism. The point is that proteins determine how the brain (and the individual) functions or at what level it functions. A major reason why protein levels change is because of changes in the activity of genes or in *gene expression*. Changing gene expression ultimately has an effect somehow, somewhere. And, as we have said, drugs of abuse cause changes in gene expression that, in the end, result in a behavioral state characterized by the urge to find and take more drugs!

It's the Molecules that Do It

The key to understanding the compulsion to take drugs begins in the synapse and the next or postsynaptic neuron (refer to Chapter 4, "The ABCs of Drug Action in the Brain," Figures 4-1 and 4-4). When drug taking results in either increases or decreases in neurotransmission, gene expression is likely to be altered. As described previously, neurotransmission involves signal transduction, which is the change that occurs in biochemical pathways inside the neuron after a receptor is stimulated. A key feature of this process is the activation of transcription factors by intracellular signaling (see Figure 5-4).

Transcription factors are proteins that interact with the parts of the genes called the promoter that controls whether or not the gene is expressed and makes proteins (see Figure 5-4). Our knowledge of transcription factors and how they interact with genes is growing. You can think of a transcription factor as the hand that touches the door knob (which is analogous to the promoter part of the gene) and turns it; the opening of the door is like an increase in gene expression. An interesting discovery has been that there are some transcription factors that build up in neurons with repeated cocaine administration. For example, Dr. Eric Nestler and colleagues discovered a transcription factor called *delta Fos-B*, whose levels incrementally increased with each cocaine injection, causing it to become more and more powerful in changing gene expression.

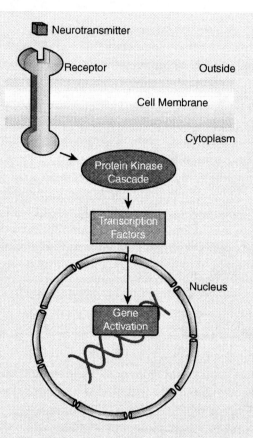

Figure 5-4   Drugs change gene expression by signal transduction. An example of the complex process of signal transduction is shown in this diagram of part of a neuron containing a receptor embedded in the cell membrane. Near the center of the nerve cell body is the nucleus with its DNA/chromosomes depicted as a double-stranded helix. The chromosomes contain the genes, some of which are activated at any given moment. On the top part of the neuron is a transmembrane receptor with a notch in the top. The transmembrane receptor is about to bind a neurotransmitter. When the neurotransmitter binds to the receptor, the receptor changes shape and activates a series of processes inside the cell referred to as a cascade, because it is a series of connected steps. The cascade activates other proteins, called transcription factors, which regulate gene expression. In other words, an activated transcription factor can turn on or shut off the expression of genes in the chromosomes. Because drugs can drastically alter the action of neurotransmitters, drugs can drastically alter gene expression through this mechanism. Also, signal transduction can produce epigenetic changes where there are alterations in the copying of the DNA. Changes in gene expression alter the biochemical makeup of the cell and therefore the function of the cell. (Image courtesy Dr. Danton O'Day, University of Toronto Mississauga.)

This understanding of how drugs change the brain has been a major achievement of the last many decades. The goal of research now is to identify the most important genes and the most significant brain regions that cause drug addiction.

An aside is that drugs can also produce other kinds of changes in brain. One of these is phosphorylation, which is adding a phosphate to various proteins, such as the phosphorylation of transcription factors, which can increase their activity. These changes are important for the effects of drugs, but the long-term changes are usually associated with changes in gene expression.

Epigenetic Changes

A change in the production of a protein is almost always due to a change in gene expression.[4] Thus far, we have discussed the ability of transcription factors to alter the expression of genes, but another way has been found in recent years. This has been referred to as Epigenetics (see the next section, "Epigenetics: A Way to Change the Brain"). Epigenetic changes occur when the environment (for example, a drug) influences our genes in a lasting way, such that some genes become inactivated, or perhaps more activated. This change in activation occurs by chemically altering the DNA itself or by changing proteins called *histones*—proteins that control access to a gene. The discovery of epigenetics explains how genetically identical individuals, but who have different experiences, can express different proteins and be different. Genetically identical twins are not always identical in all ways. Moreover, epigenetics explains another way that drug taking can influence gene expression.

Epigenetics: A Way to Change the Brain

An epigenetic change causes a change in gene expression, but it does not involve a mutation which is a change in the sequence of chemical bases in the DNA (see Figure 5-3). Rather, it involves a chemical modification of either the DNA or the proteins surrounding the DNA such that gene expression is changed.

When addicting drugs enter the brain, they alter chemical neurotransmission (Figure 5-3), and produce epigenetic changes
that influence gene expression, and hence modify the biochemical makeup of the brain.

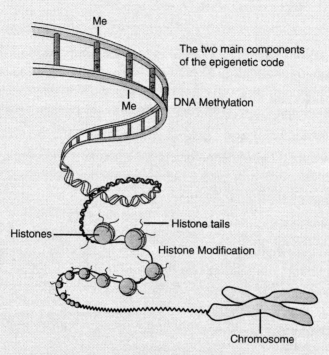

This figure shows the unraveling of a chromosome near the bottom and how DNA is stored in the chromosome. The DNA,
which contains our genes, is wrapped around proteins called
histones to provide an efficient storage of the DNA in the tiny
nucleus of the cell. Near the top is the standard, double
stranded model of DNA. Epigenetic modification includes two
main mechanisms. One is methylating the DNA, which changes
its ability to make protein, and the other is modifying the histones, which change the way DNA is accessed and translated
into protein. Both procedures can be affected by drugs.
(From http://www.lexic.us/definition-of/epigenetic, accessed on
January 15, 2001.)

In any case, mechanisms aside, it is clear that drug taking can influence the biochemical makeup of the brain. This is the molecular heart of addiction.

Postmortem Findings

When the brains from addicts that have died are analyzed (referred to as postmortem studies),[5] there are many biochemicals whose levels are changed. It still is not clear which chemicals and brain regions are the most significant for drug addiction, but we have many hints. It is likely that changes in many chemicals and many neurons (as opposed to one chemical in one neuron) are required for the addiction process. So, although we don't know the full story, we have at least the beginnings of a story.

Postmortem studies have been carried out in several species including man. In general, the results point out many neuroplastic changes that amount to significant impairments in neuronal function. Receptors, such as D2 dopamine receptors and glutamate receptors, signaling proteins, proteins involved in energy metabolism, and proteins involved in cell structure were found to be changed by drug use.[6] Proteins are large molecules that are chains of amino acids and can have many uses in the cell, from being receptors to being transporters. But, the exact proteins that are changed might depend on the drug that is studied. This approach to looking at multiple brain changes in biochemical assays is somewhat easier and cheaper than imaging approaches, which usually focus on just one biochemical, such as a dopamine receptor, at a time.

Although studying the effects of drugs on human brains is a direct approach to the problem, there are limitations with studying humans. One is that most drug users are multi-drug users, so we don't know which drug is producing the effects. Also, drug users are not noted for taking good care of their health and perhaps the poor health is producing the changes in the brain and not the drugs. Yet another issue is that many drug users have a simultaneous diagnosis of a mental disorder, and maybe the mental disorder is producing the changes. So, in any study of drug users, these problems have to be addressed, and this is done by selecting a control group who has similar problems without the drug use, as best as we can. As a result, caution is essential when interpreting the results. For these and other reasons, studies with animals are helpful because we can control many more factors, such as lifetime nutrition and drug use, than we can in humans.

Drug Use Changes the Activity of the Brain

It isn't surprising, given that drugs change the biochemical makeup of the brain and that drugs change the electrical and metabolic activity patterns in the brain. This was clearly shown by Dr. Linda Porrino and her colleagues who analyzed glucose utilization in monkeys after a few initial doses of cocaine and after many doses (chronic) of cocaine. Glucose utilization is relevant because the parts of the brain that use more glucose do so because they are more active and therefore need more energy. The brain slices shown in Figure 5-5 have dark regions showing where glucose utilization was high. Note that the area of high glucose utilization was enlarged in the slice from an animal treated chronically with cocaine compared to the slice from an animal with only an initial experience with the drug (see Figure 5-5). It is as though drugs take over more and more of the brain gradually, and their influence spreads. Figure 5-5 shows only one slice of brain but the study revealed that many regions of the brain responded to drugs by enlarging the regions of glucose utilization. This is a nice demonstration of the power and influence of drugs on the brain, and, ultimately, on behavior.

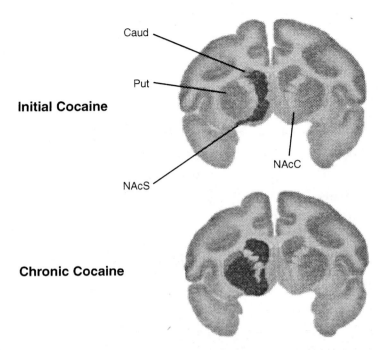

Figure 5-5   More and more drug taking changes more and more of the brain. Slices of brain show regions of high glucose utilization by the dark color. Glucose utilization, or energy consumption, by the brain increased in specific areas (that are identified) after chronic cocaine administration. See text for more details. Caud = caudate nucleus, Put = putamen, NAcS = nucleus accumbens shell, NAcC = nucleus accumbens core. These brain regions are important in drug addiction. (From L.J. Porrino, H.R. Smith, M.A. Nader and T.J. Beveridge. "The Effects of Cocaine: A Shifting Target over the Course of Addiction." *Prog in Neuropsychopharmacol and Biol Psychiat*, 31:1593-1600. Copyright [2007]), with permission from Elsevier.)

Summary

Addiction occurs after repeated drug taking. This is so because chronic drug taking alters chemical neurotransmission and cellular signaling, which in turn changes the brain by altering gene expression and the proteins that are made. As drug taking continues, the drug begins to influence larger and larger portions of the brain. When the drug is no longer present, the changed brain is out of balance and withdrawal symptoms occur. Repeated drug taking also produces the adaptive changes of tolerance and sensitization.

Endnotes

1   This is summarized from a *New York Times* article that appeared August 30, 2010, and was written by Richard Friedman MD, entitled "Lasting pleasures, robbed by drug abuse."

2   Plasticity, or neuroplasticity, is the ability of the brain to change in response to a stimulus. In the context here, it is the ability of the functions of the brain to change in response to drugs. Plastic changes can be an increase or decrease in the number of synaptic connections in the brain, or in changes in the levels of important proteins. Tolerance and addiction involve plasticity. Dr. Antonello Bonci and others have reviewed some of the findings on plasticity in Stuber G.D. et al. *Curr Top Behav Neurosci*, 3:3–27., 2010, and in Chen B.T. et al. *Ann N Y Acad Sci*, 1187:129–139, 2010.

3   Ibid.

4   Normally, changes in gene expression are defined by changes in the level of mRNA, which is made directly from DNA (see Figure 5-2). However, for the sake of simplicity, we often define proteins as the product of gene expression.

5   Endnote 1 in Chapter 2, "Hardwired: What Animals Tell Us About the Human Desire for Drugs," describes how human subjects in research protocols must be protected against risk. These rules apply even in postmortem studies. For example, the identities of the subjects must be concealed in any discussion of or publication of data from the use of the brain tissue.

6   For example, see Hemby, S.E. "Cocainomics: New Insights into the Molecular Basis of Cocaine Addiction." *J Neuroimmune Pharmacol*, 5:70–82, 2010. Flatscher-Bader T. et al. "Comparative Gene Expression in Brain Regions of Human Alcoholics." *Genes Brain Behav*, 5 (Suppl 1):78–84, 2006.

6

Why Are Drugs So Powerful?

Arla, like other members of her family, is a bright, attractive, and successful person. She's always been popular and a leader in many activities. As you might expect, she's confident of her abilities and feels that she can succeed at anything she really tries. But, she has a secret and a worry. She has been taking opiate drugs, at first for pain from a root canal, for many months. She has come to crave the high and has discovered that even though she really wants to and tries to stop, she relapses to drug use after a couple of weeks at most. She is beginning to worry that she might need help stopping, but she doesn't really want to admit this, because it seems like a failure. She can't believe that her urge is so powerful.

Why are drugs so powerful that some people lose control of their actions to some degree? People can become sociopaths, liars, and destructive to their loved ones, all in a compulsion to find and take drugs. Certainly this does not happen to everyone who tries drugs, but it happens to enough people that it is considered a national problem. Note that this is not asking why drugs *cause* addiction, but rather why is addiction itself so *powerful*. This is an important question that we haven't fully answered, but we do have some ideas about it.

One reason that drugs are so powerful has been described in Chapter 4, "The ABCs of Drug Action in the Brain." They enter the brain and dominate the process of chemical neurotransmission, and the brain by itself doesn't have any ways to fight that domination.

Drugs, therefore, can "push the brain around" and override natural processes. But we think there might be other reasons as well. There are some additional hypotheses about the power of drugs that are based on specific circuits and brain regions that contribute to our survival and living. Neuronal circuits that contain dopamine are good examples of this.

The dopaminergic mesolimbic system, which is an important substrate for drugs in the brain, evolved in our brains over many millions of years. Why is it there, and what exactly does dopamine do? The answers to these questions have developed over the years and are probably not yet complete. An early view was that release of dopamine was like turning on a switch that told you when something felt good and should be repeated. In other words, dopamine is rewarding because it makes us feel good when we have a nice meal or make love. Dopamine is also reinforcing because it motivates you to repeat certain actions, such as eating and sex, which are important for survival—not only for the survival of the individual, but also for the survival of the species!

Dopamine and Food

There is abundant evidence that dopamine is associated with fundamentally important actions, such as food intake and mating.[1] Figure 6-1 shows a schematic of the human brain and neuronal pathways that contain dopaminergic neurons. The names of the anatomical regions are unfortunately a bit arcane, and derive from historical discoveries and Latin. But decades of scientific work has shown that these dopamine-containing neurons are involved in many functions surrounding feeding and sexual behavior.

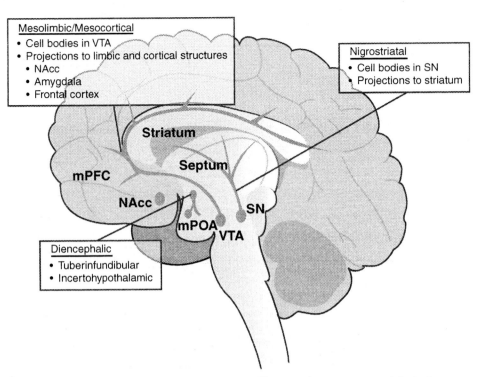

Figure 6-1   Brain dopamine (DA) systems. Three major systems contribute to sexual arousal and desire, including the mesolimbic and mesocortical DA system. This system has DA-containing cell bodies in the ventral tegmental area (VTA) with terminals in the nucleus accumbens (NAcc) (and other limbic regions) and medial prefrontal cortex (mPFC), respectively. Other DA systems shown include the diencephalic system and the nigrostriatal system. The tuberoinfundibular DA system controls hormone release from the anterior pituitary gland. These systems control attention and motivation related to sexual and feeding stimuli and are also involved in the regulation of mood and emotions, attention, motivation, reward and reinforcement, and the actions of cocaine. SN = substantia nigra; mPOA = medial preoptic area. (From "Figure 3" from Pfaus, James G., "Reviews: Pathways of Sexual Desire," *Journal of Sexual Medicine*, Copyright © 2009. Reprinted with permission of John Wiley & Sons, Inc.)

A few experimental findings can be mentioned to support this. Food intake is associated with a release of dopamine in the nucleus accumbens, a place in the brain involved in addiction. In bulimic subjects, for example, dopamine metabolites in the brain fluids, which reflect the amount of dopamine used at the synapse, suggested a reduced activity of dopaminergic neurons in subjects with this eating disorder. Another more complicated kind of evidence comes from molecular biology and genetics. It has been discussed how important the dopamine transporter is for normal dopaminergic neurotransmission. Like many proteins, there are several naturally occurring variants of the transporter gene that are inherited by various individuals. One molecular variant of the dopamine transporter is more often found in people who binge, suggesting a genetic linkage between the dopamine system and binge eating (see the next section, "The Dopamine Transporter Is Connected to Binge Eating"). Other work in animal studies have related compulsive eating with dopamine,[2] and D2 dopamine receptors are reduced in both humans and animals that are obese.

The Dopamine Transporter Is Connected to Binge Eating

Genes are the units of heredity that determine the features of our bodies. Also, genes can undergo mutations, and, as you know, some mutations are not friendly and can produce disease, whereas others have only neutral or subtle effects. The collection of genes in our chromosomes is called the genome, and each of us, because of the way in which we inherit genes from our parents, have unique genomes, but of course we share many features of our family's genome.

There are genetic mutations that result in rearrangements, deletions, or even in repetitions of parts of the genome. One situation where there are repetitions of genes is referred to as a variable number tandem repeat (VNTR). This means that different individuals can have different or variable numbers of genes that are repeated. In other words, I might have nine copies of the dopamine transporter gene lined up in a row next to each other (that is what tandem means), whereas you might have ten copies. In the schematic that follows, you can see four different tandem repeats where a gene (the elongated rectangle) is repeated six, four, three, or five times.

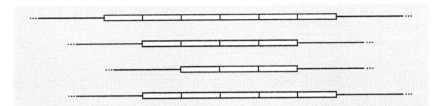

This is important because the number of repeats can affect the way the gene is expressed, which can have effects on human health. In other words, someone with nine repeats instead of ten might be more susceptible to a health problem. Also, it is important because the VNTRs can be used as genetic markers to study heritability patterns.

In a study of patients with a binge-eating disorder, it was determined that the fewer number of VNTRs was found more frequently in the subjects with the binge-eating disorder (Shinohara et al. *J Psychiatr Neurosci* 29:134-137, 2004). Thus, a modification of the transporter gene has significant effects on our eating and presumably drug-taking behavior. (Schematic from http://en.wikipedia.org/wiki/Variable_number_tandem_ repeat, accessed September 27, 2010.)

Regarding interactions between eating and taking drugs, Drs. Ken Carr, Marilyn Carroll, David Gorelick, and others have shown in animals and humans that caloric restrictions (in other words, dieting) result in greater drug intake.[3] For example, in humans, dieting was associated with a small but significant increase in nicotine delivery by cigarette smoking.

Dopamine and Sexual Behavior

Regarding sexual behavior and dopamine, it has long been known that, for example, injections of dopamine-related drugs into the hypothalamus of laboratory animals can influence the interaction between male and female rats and the number of ejaculations produced by the male. Another experiment has associated sexual activity with dopamine in the nucleus accumbens, a brain region well known to be connected to drugs. The far left side of Figure 6-2 shows the dopamine levels in the brain of a male animal when he is undisturbed in his home cage during the first 20 minutes of the experiment. When you transfer the animal to the test chamber, the levels rise slightly, and they rise slightly again when he is placed in the cage together with a receptive female. But dopamine levels go way up with copulation (shown as male and female together, around 90–120 minutes), and after the female is removed, dopamine levels decline. Because dopamine levels go up in the same brain region when we take drugs (for example, refer to Figure 4-5 in Chapter 4), the brain, in a sense, sees drugs and sex as the same. Drugs are as powerful as sex and some drug users report that the rush from taking some drugs is like a whole body orgasm. Quite amazing (also refer to Figure 4-5)!

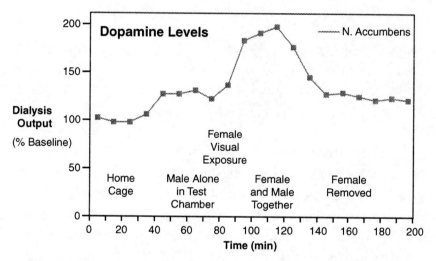

Figure 6-2   Mating results in dopamine release. Dopamine levels (a measure of dopamine release by neurons), indicated by "dialysis output" on the vertical axis, increased when the male rat was placed in a novel chamber and again when a receptive female was introduced. A subsequent copulation resulted in a sharp increase of dopamine release. Dopamine levels returned to normal after the female was removed from the chamber. Dopamine levels also went up in the brain after rats received an injection of cocaine (refer to Figure 4-5). From the point of view of the brain and the neuron receiving dopamine, the brain doesn't know whether the animal had cocaine or copulated. (Adapted from J.G. Pfaus, G. Damsma, G.G. Nomikos, D.G. Wenkstern, C.D. Blaha, A.G. Philips and H.C. Fibiger. Sexual behavior enhances central dopamine transmission in the male rat. *Brain Res*, 530:345-348. 1990, with permission from Elsevier.)

In a study of human subjects who had recently fallen in love, there were activations in the ventral tegmental area, part of the dopamine mesolimbic system. In studies of male orgasms, the ventral tegmental area was one of the regions activated.[4] In a paper entitled "Prelude to passion; limbic activation by 'unseen' drug and sexual cues," Drs. Anna Rose Childress, Charles O'Brien, and others from the University of Pennsylvania found that there was limbic activation in subjects that received cues about drugs and sex outside of their awareness.[5] The brain can receive short signals that are outside of our conscious recognition, and those are referred to as "unseen" cues; the paper shows that brain reward circuitry responds to these unseen cues. This demonstrates an interesting, additional vulnerability of the brain to drugs and other stimuli.

A major point here is that elevations in dopamine and activations of dopaminergic areas are associated with powerful urges, such as the sexual drive to mate, which is critical for survival of the species. The increased dopamine is associated with something that feels good, or with something that you want to do again and again.

Dopamine and Survival

Given what has been discussed, it seems justified to propose that the dopamine mesolimbic system is important for survival and is part of "survival pathways" in the brain for both individuals and the species. Without these pathways, perhaps our species would not survive or survive as well. In fact, special transgenic mice have been prepared that do not have dopamine in the brain. When these dopamine-depleted animals are born, they do not move or eat normally and die by four weeks of age.[6] If the survival pathways in the brain have more power over behavior than other pathways, and if drugs work by inserting themselves in those pathways, then drugs will have relatively more power over our behavior (see Endnote 2 in Chapter 4). Therefore, drugs are powerful at least partly because they work through powerful brain circuits. Although this is a hypothesis and one can argue about the meaning of the word powerful, this seems to be a reasonable position.

If this hypothesis is true, then it might explain some other puzzling issues. For one thing, if drug addiction is bad, and it obviously is, then why hasn't it been weeded out by evolution? Given the survival hypothesis, it hasn't been weeded out because it is intrinsically connected to survival functions like eating and mating. Addiction hooks into mechanisms for natural rewards, and genetic mutations that blunt addictions would have a negative survival impact.

One can argue that all parts of the brain and their functions are just as critical for individual and species survival as the mesolimbic dopamine system, but this doesn't seem to be true. When it comes to survival of the species, sex is the main factor. For survival of the individual, it seems there are many factors but food is definitely a major one. Loss of movement, sensory detection, and focus are also critical for survival, but you can argue that they are a means to locate and get to food. Also, people survive with losses of many of these functions. In any case, there are many important parts of the brain but the dopamine mesolimbic system, along with additional connecting neurons in the circuitry, seems to be paramount for basic survival brain functions.

Not Only Dopamine

But it wouldn't be accurate to imply that dopamine and its neurons are the sole, powerful players here for all drugs. Dopamine is a major player for drugs such as opiates and psychostimulants, like cocaine and amphetamine. But there are other neurons, circuits, and neurotransmitters in the picture that we have not mentioned or explored.[7] For example, Dr. Peter Kalivas, his colleagues, and others have shown that molecular changes in a neuronal pathway from the prefrontal cortex to the nucleus accumbens core underlie cocaine seeking, and this circuit uses the neurotransmitter glutamate.[8] It is not just the effects of drugs on a given neurotransmitter, but also the impact of drugs on the specific circuits, brain regions, and their functions that are important as well. Dopamine was used as an example to bring out the idea that the specific functional pathways in the brain that drugs attack are at least partially responsible for the power of drugs.

But it is interesting to consider other drugs, because it is sometimes possible to relate their actions to the action of dopamine in the nucleus accumbens and to circuits containing dopamine. Self-administration of nicotine, which mimics the neurotransmitter acetylcholine, and acts at receptors for acetylcholine, also results in an increase in the release of dopamine in the nucleus accumbens, a drug reward area. Thus, the mesolimbic dopaminergic pathway is involved with nicotine/smoking even though the directly affected neurotransmitter is acetylcholine and not dopamine. But, nicotine probably uses additional mechanisms and pathways.[9] Although dopamine has been implicated in the addicting action of many drugs, not all drugs have been conclusively connected to dopamine at this time.

What Does Dopamine Do?

This is a question with which scientists have struggled. It's been said that dopamine is associated with pleasure or reward. After all, it looks that way, and brain imaging studies in humans, for example, have associated dopamine levels with the high and euphoria produced by the drug.[10] But, dopamine is not just there for pleasure! Addicts are not in a constant state of pleasure, and animal studies show that dopamine levels increase in the face of fear.[11] So the concept of what dopamine does has had to evolve.

A more recent view is that dopamine tells us or signals to us what is *salient*, meaning what is arousing or alerting, and this is linked to motivation.[12] Dopamine alerts us or arouses us not only to the availability of food and sex, but also to impending danger and pain. According to this idea, the salience due to dopamine can be considered an alerting sensory act like tasting or listening. From this point of view, drug users are not simply seeking pleasure, and the lack of pleasure in addiction has been observed and reported by addicts.

Summary

Drug addiction is obviously a powerful brain disorder that can drive our behavior in spite of personal distress and negative consequences. Drugs are powerful partly because the brain does not have mechanisms to control their levels and drugs can therefore overpower the brain. But it is hypothesized that drugs are also powerful because of the parts of the brain that they act in. For example, cocaine blocks the removal of dopamine from the synapse by blocking the dopamine transporter, thereby increasing dopaminergic neurotransmission. This happens in dopaminergic neurons (mesolimbic neurons) that are part of circuits in the brain associated with feeding, sex, and other important life-sustaining processes. Therefore, the constant "battering" of the dopamine system in the brain by repeated cocaine use causes adjustments and adaptations over time in a brain system driving vital behaviors. However, these systems, even though altered by drugs, can still profoundly influence our behavior, although in an altered and abnormal way. Dopamine is not only involved in pleasure, but also in alerting and motivation. A difference is that the object of desire now becomes cocaine (or another drug) instead of a natural reward. From this perspective, drug addiction is a disorder or disease of motivation. Other neurotransmitters such as glutamate and acetylcholine are also involved in drug addiction.

Endnotes

[1] There are several excellent and relatively recent review articles summarizing the data showing a role for dopamine in natural rewards such as sexual behavior and feeding. These include Baskerville, T.A. and A.J. Douglas. "Dopamine and Oxytocin Interactions Underlying Behaviors." *CNS Neurosci Ther,* 16:92–123, 2010. Pfaus J.G. "Pathways of Sexual Desire." *J Sex Med,* 6:1506–1533, 2009. Kelley, A.E. "Ventral Striatal Control of Appetitive Motivation." *Neurosci Behav Rev,* 27:765–776, 2004.

Carlezon, W.A. and M.J. Thomas. "Biological Substrates of Reward and Aversion." *Neuropharmacol*, 56 suppl 1:122–132, 2009. Peeters, M. and F. Giulliano. "Central Neurophysiology and Dopaminergic Control of Ejaculation." *Neurosci Biobehav Rev*, 32:438–453, 2008.

2 Bello, N.T. and A. Hajnal. "Dopamine and Binge Eating Behaviors." *Pharmacol Biochem Behav*, 97: 25–33, 2010.

3 Examples of these studies can be found in Cheskin L.J. et al. "Calorie Restriction Increases Cigarette Use in Adult Smokers." *Psychopharmacology*, 179:430–436, 2004. Carr, K.D. et al. "Chronic Food Restriction in Rats Augments the Central Rewarding Effect of Cocaine..." *Psychopharmacology*, 152: 200–207, 2000. Carroll, M.E. "Interactions between Food and Addiction." In Niesink, R.J.M., Jaspers RMA, Kornet L.M.W., and J.M. van Ree (eds) *"Drugs of Abuse and Addiction: Neurobehavioral Toxicology."* CRC, Boca Raton, pp 286–311,1998.

4 Summarized in D.J. Linden *The Accidental Mind*, Harvard University Press, 2007. page 162.

5 Paper in *PLoS ONE*, 3(1): e1506, January 2008. doi:10.1371/journal.pone.0001506.

6 Zhou Q.Y. and R.D. Palmiter. "Dopamine-Deficient Mice Are Severely Hypoactive, Adipsic, and Aphagic." *Cell*, 83:1197–1209, 1995.

7 Neurons containing the neurotransmitters GABA or acetylcholine are important for addiction to alcohol or nicotine. (Interestingly, these influence the release of or the action of dopamine in the nucleus accumbens.)

8 The Kalivas model deals with glutamate-containing neurons that project from the prefrontal cortex to the nucleus accumbens and that regulate dopamine release. Dopamine facilitates learning of adaptations to important stimuli. This prefrontal cortex neural

pathway regulates seeking behaviors such as drug addiction, and it is impaired by drug use. Repeated cocaine use results in molecular changes in this pathway. A recent review is Kalivas, P.W. and C. O'Brien. "Drug Addiction as a Pathology of Staged Neuroplasticity." *Neuropsychopharmacology Reviews* 33:166–180, 2008.

[9]   Koob, G.F. and M. Le Moal. Chapter 6, "Nicotine." *Neurobiology of Addiction,* Elsevier, 2006.

[10] Volkow, N.D. et al. "Imaging Dopamine's Role in Drug Abuse and Addiction." *Neuropharmacol,* 56 (Suppl 1) 3–8, 2009.

[11] Badgaiyan, R.D. et al. "Dopamine Release During Human Emotional Processing," *Neuroimage,* 47:2041-5, 2009. Martinez, R.C. et al. "Involvement of Dopaminergic Mechanisms in the Nu-cleus Accumbens Core and Shell Subregions in the Expression of Fear Conditioning," *Neurosci Lett,* 446:112–116, 2008. Levita, L. et al. "Nucleus Accumbens Dopamine and Learned Fear Revisited: A Review and Some New Findings." *Behav Brain Res,* 137:115–127, 2002.

[12] Berridge, K.C. "The Debate over Dopamine's Role in Reward: The Case for Incentive Salience." *Psychopharmacol,* 191:391–43.1, 2007.

7

The Brain Is Changed—
For a Long Time!

"Before I started drugs, I did great. I never had a hang-up like this. I can't seem to get over wanting drugs, no matter how hard I try. I stay away from the stuff for weeks, but it doesn't seem to make a difference. I keep going back."

Why is drug addiction so long lasting? Just because drugs exert *powerful* actions in the brain doesn't mean that their effects should last a *long time*. But they do! How do we study this?

Looking at the Drug User's Brain

Brain imaging is a remarkably powerful tool that enables us to peer inside the skull and brain (see Figure 7-1), and measure various quantities associated with neurotransmission and drugs. There are various types of imaging that tell us different things. Positron Emission Tomography (PET) scanning[1] can measure both the levels of some proteins (such as receptors) and their levels of activity as well as glucose metabolism in certain regions (see "PET Scanning").

PET Scanning

Positron Emission Tomography (PET) is an imaging technique that produces a three-dimensional picture of the distribution of a radioactive substance in the body. If the substance is preferentially bound to some receptor, for example, then the distribution of radioactivity shows the distribution and quantity of the receptors. If the radioactivity reflects metabolism, then the distribution of radioactivity shows areas that are highly metabolic or functional. PET is one of the most important research tools available today. It allows us to look inside the body for important molecules and processes without invading the tissues of the body. PET can also be combined with other powerful imaging techniques such as CT and MRI to provide even more information.

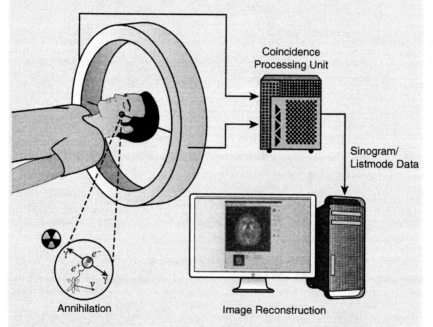

This schematic shows how PET scanning works. If a radioactive substance that emits positrons and binds preferentially to D2 dopamine receptors, for example, is injected into a subject, then the substance will settle onto D2 receptors in the brain. As the positrons are emitted during radioactive decay, they encounter electrons, and, being antiparticles, they annihilate each other and produce gamma radiation (see lower left) that is detected by a ring of detectors arranged around the head. The information about the annihilations is then processed and sent to a computer where the spatial distribution of the radioactivity (and the receptors) is reconstructed.

Image adapted from "Positron Emission Tomography," in http://en.wikipedia.org/wiki/Positron_emission_tomography, accessed November 18, 2010.)

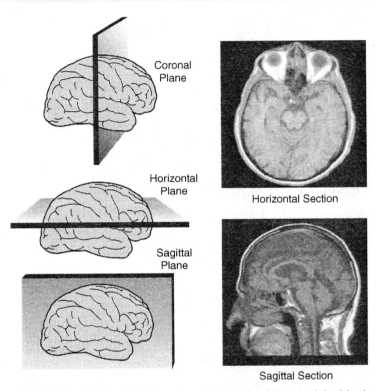

Coronal Plane

Horizontal Plane

Horizontal Section

Sagittal Plane

Sagittal Section

Figure 7-1   Understanding brain images. Imaging machines look inside the head and brain and display slices of the brain. The schematic on the left shows three different ways or planes that the human brain can be sliced in. Sometimes structures of interest are better seen in one plane or another. Brain imaging instruments look at slices of the brain and reconstruct them so that the details of structure (or function) can be seen, as on the right. The images on the right were obtained using magnetic resonance imaging (MRI). Although the schematic images on the left show only the brain, the actual brain images shown on the right include the skull, eyes, nose, and other tissues, which are more realistic. The PET images shown in Figures 7-2 and 7-3 are horizontal sections that reveal the distribution of radioactivity in slices of the brain. (Adapted from http://faculty.washington.edu/chudler/slice.html.)

Studies using brain-imaging techniques have shown that continued use of drugs causes long-lasting changes in brain chemistry and function. For example, dopamine receptors, specifically the D2 type of receptor, are decreased in the brains of drug abusers who take cocaine, methamphetamine, alcohol, or heroin. When an established addict stops taking cocaine or some other drugs, the D2 dopamine receptor levels do not immediately increase to normal (see Figure 7-2). In fact, they remain suppressed for months and months, and this has proven to be the case in several studies. The low levels of the receptors have suggested that the dopamine system is dysfunctional or under-functioning in these people. In other studies, low D2 levels were also found in obese subjects, echoing the importance of dopamine in "natural" rewards, and that drugs insert themselves in circuits for natural rewards such as feeding. Thus, low levels of D2 dopamine receptors are a suggestive marker for increased vulnerability to drug use, and perhaps other addictive behaviors as well.

Because of the long-lasting changes in receptors (and presumably many other proteins), the brains of addicts will function differently for a long time.[2] In fact, imaging studies clearly show long-lasting changes in brain function in addition to changes in protein levels. Figure 7-3 shows that taking cocaine for a long time causes significant changes in energy metabolism (a measure of function) in the brain. Levels of energy metabolism (indicated by light areas in the image) are compared in a normal subject, a cocaine user who has not taken cocaine for 10 days, and one who has not taken cocaine for 100 days. It is clear that even after 100 days of abstinence, the brain has not returned to normal.

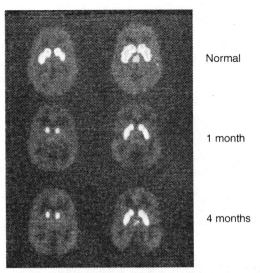

Normal

1 month

4 months

Figure 7-2   Levels of D2 dopamine receptors in a normal brain (top), a brain from a cocaine user after one month of withdrawal (middle), and a brain from a cocaine user after four months of withdrawal (bottom). Each row shows two different slices of brain from the same subject and comparisons are made by examining the images in each column. The bright areas in the image show the places where D2 dopamine receptors are the highest—the larger the brighter area, the greater the number of receptors. For example, consider the left column that shows the same brain levels from three individuals, one with no drug history and two users. The top image from an individual with no drug history has the most receptors, the middle image from a user abstinent for one month has many fewer receptors, and the third or lowest level shows perhaps a slightly higher level compared to the middle image. But it is clear that even after four months of abstinence, D2 dopamine receptor levels are not back to normal. The images are from PET scans of D2 dopamine receptors, which were first carried out a team of which the author was a member. (Adapted from "Figure 2" from Volkow et al. "Decreased Dopamine D2 Receptor Availability Is Associated with Reduced Frontal Metabolism in Cocaine Abusers," Synapse, 14:169–177, 1993, with permission of John Wiley & Sons, Inc.)

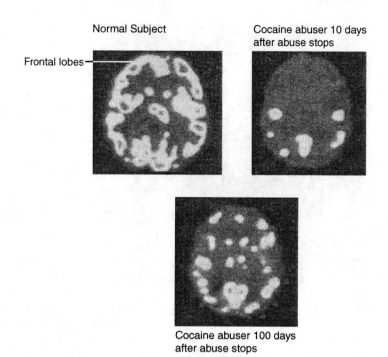

Figure 7-3   Energy metabolism is changed in abstinent cocaine abusers for months. The more lightly colored areas are regions of higher energy metabolism. The changes are notable in the frontal lobes, the brain regions where impulses are regulated. These experiments were carried out using PET scanning after injecting a radioactive form of glucose. The regions with higher levels of radioactivity show the brain regions where metabolism and neuronal activity are higher. (Courtesy of NIH/NIDA and adapted from *Time Magazine*, page 45, July 16, 2007.)

Many investigators have also found changes in animals' dopamine receptors and transporters after administering drugs. These studies often used another breakthrough technique referred to as *in vitro labeling autoradiography of receptors*, which was developed in the author's laboratory at The Johns Hopkins University School of Medicine in the late 1970s.[3] When the same results are found using different techniques, species, and approaches, there is much greater confidence in the results.

Why Such a Slow Recovery?

This is an interesting question, but the answer is not yet known. Levels or amounts of protein are interesting and informative because more protein results in more function, less protein results in less function, and also because changes in proteins point out where the effects of drugs are taking place. How do changes in proteins occur? It is perhaps obvious that the levels or amount of any given protein in the brain (or in any organ) are due to a balance between the synthesis and degradation rates of the protein. Protein levels can increase due to an increase in synthesis or to a decrease in degradation, or both. All proteins "turn over," meaning that they are used, worn out, and then replaced by new protein.[4] Let's consider this in a more graphic fashion. If we were able to label every protein molecule in our brain at any given moment with a small flag, we can watch this turnover and replacement because the new proteins will not have a flag. The time it takes for half of the flagged proteins to be replaced by new ones is called the *half life*. Every protein has an existing synthesis rate and degradation rate, and drugs can change them.

The time that it takes a protein to reach a new level after a change in synthesis or degradation depends on the *speed* of the changes in synthesis or degradation. For example, proteins that increase their levels more quickly are synthesized more quickly, degraded more slowly, or both. This is interesting because we scientists think we know something about protein synthesis and degradation and therefore have some ideas about why some protein changes in the brain can last a long time. Moreover, and importantly, we can examine whether there are worthwhile experiments where we can reduce recovery time for addicts by creating conditions in the brain where proteins change their levels more rapidly! For example, if D2 dopamine receptors are resistant or slow to change their levels in drug addicts, as experiments show, then their synthesis rate might be relatively fast and their degradation rate relatively slow. Thus, we can begin to think about whether or not we can control synthesis or degradation rates, perhaps by new medications. If we could normalize D2 receptor levels more quickly, would this help the addict recover more quickly? As intriguing as this sounds, the technologies currently available in protein biochemistry are not yet advanced enough to produce a medication that would be *selective* in changing the synthesis or degradation of a single protein such as D2 receptors. But, it is useful that we have some general idea as to what controls the levels of D2 receptors in brain and this knowledge might be helpful in the future. However, this general answer about synthesis and degradation is not good enough. We need to find out more about why certain, specific brain changes are so long lasting.

There are other possible answers to this question. Gene expression, which ultimately influences the synthesis rates of proteins, and can be altered by drugs, might be altered for a long time by drugs. This could occur because of epigenetic changes or by long-lasting changes in levels of transcription factors, which regulate genes (Chapter 5, "The Dark Side Develops!").

So What Can We Do? How Does This Help a Drug User?

Discovering that drugs change the brain for a long time is one of the most important discoveries in the field. Even though we still don't know how to treat the brain so that the changes revert to normal more quickly or even how to prevent the changes, this knowledge has a big impact in many ways. *First*, it helps us understand the problem of drug addiction in a basic and mechanistic way. The duration of the changes explain why drug addiction appears to be chronic, and it seems likely that a lack of appreciation of this contributes to relapse. *Second*, it defines a critical problem in the research laboratory—how exactly do the changes occur and how can we block or reverse them? If we can block or reverse the brain processes that underlie addiction, then we can treat addicts better. *Third*, just knowing that the brain is changed for a long time tells addicts that recovery is going to be a slow process, lasting months. If they know that they will be vulnerable for a long time after cessation, they will hopefully be more vigilant and stay away from drugs during this dangerous time. *Fourth*, the addict's support system, which is usually made up of friends, family, and treatment providers, now know that vulnerability to relapse lasts many months and the addict will need a support system that extends in time. Novel treatment paradigms that provide long-term support might be needed. *Fifth*, lawmakers and policy makers that regulate treatment and payments for treatment are now informed that this brain disorder/illness lasts a long time. Would you want reimbursement from insurance for only one day of antibiotics if a known type of infection takes seven days to eliminate? Of course not. Hopefully, not all effective long-term treatments have to be expensive. As you can see, understanding and dealing with the long-term effects of addiction is challenging on many fronts!

Does the Brain Ever Get Back to Normal?

After someone has been an addict, does his or her brain ever normalize? This is one of the most important questions in the field. Some believe that at least some of the changes caused by drugs last forever, which if true, will impact treatment. Although evidence is still accumulating, there are some findings that we can examine. Twelve-step programs such as those used by Alcoholics Anonymous and Narcotics Anonymous assume that addicts have a chronic disease and chronic vulnerability. Using this assumption, these programs suggest that addiction is never cured, but can be treated by avoiding drugs. This is perhaps the safest approach to treatment. These programs have an effective track record with effective procedures. Perhaps some brains carry a chronic vulnerability that can't be completely reversed, and perhaps some can be changed by treatment. Additional research is needed to discuss this question in a more informed way.

An interesting study by Dr. Michael Nader and his colleagues at Wake Forest University looked at the recovery of D2 dopamine receptors in the brains of five monkeys.[5] When the animals self-administered cocaine for some time, their levels of D2 receptors dropped as expected (low D2 levels reflect a propensity to take drugs). The receptor levels were then monitored after cessation of cocaine use for the next 12 months. In three of the five animals, the receptors returned to normal levels by three months (this seems to be faster than it happens in humans). But in two of the monkeys, the levels did not return to normal even after 12 months! So there were individual differences in the monkeys in that some reverted to normal and some didn't. This is just like humans. Individual differences in human drug users have long been noted as important. Based on this study's results, you see that all drug users are not the same and treatment has to be flexible to take into account individual differences.

Here is an anecdote from my own history. As a young man, I smoked tobacco for years. But, when a relative died of lung cancer, I decided to stop smoking—and much to my surprise (it shouldn't have been)—I craved tobacco for a long time! The second six months of abstinence produced worse craving than the first six months (at least it seemed that way). I especially craved when others smoked after a meal, which was the time when I enjoyed smoking the most. Sometimes I would even get up and leave the table so I wouldn't be affected by others' lighting up. After about a year, the craving for tobacco began to reduce, and after about 18 months, I experienced no craving at all. Today, many years later, smoking bothers my throat and lungs and leaves me coughing, and I consider myself totally cured of that addiction. Because of this, I feel that addiction is curable (at least in my case). Still, I can't be absolutely sure that there isn't some residue of change left in my brain that somehow increases my vulnerability to relapse. If there is some lasting change in my brain, it doesn't seem significant at all. Take note, however, that this single story does not minimize the fact that many drug users might crave for longer times or might never stop taking drugs.

Summary

Drugs change the biochemical makeup of the brain for a long time, and the changes persist long after one stops taking drugs. This presumably explains why drug addiction appears to be a chronic and relapsing disease. Laboratory research has shown that this finding can be understood in terms of drugs causing changes in levels of functionally important proteins. The mechanisms that drugs might use can include epigenetic changes or other changes in gene regulation. However this limited understanding needs substantial improvement. The realization that the brain changes for a long time has had a major impact on our goals and methods for developing and delivering treatments. Because the duration of the changes might be different for different drug users, the ability of an individual drug user to recover from addiction might require a custom-made treatment program.

Endnotes

[1] The development of PET scanning as we know it today took more than half a century. The concept of emission and transmission tomography was introduced by David Kuhl and Roy Edwards in the late 1950s. Tomography is producing images of sections of the body through the use of any kind of penetrating wave (such as gamma radiation). Michel Ter-Pogossian and Michael E. Phelps at Washington University School of Medicine, and Gordon Brownell and Charles Burham at Mass General, also made significant advances in PET technology. However, it was Al Wolfe and Joanna Fowler at Brookhaven National Labs that contributed to the acceptance of PET by the development of 2-fluorodeoxy-D-glucose—a chemical that is used to measure metabolism in the brain. They, along with Abass Alavi at the University of Pennsylvania, showed how PET can be used to monitor activity in the brain. PET scanning of receptors in the brain was developed at Johns Hopkins in the early 1980s by a team lead by Henry

Wagner. Mike Kuhar, the author, was a senior member of the team who had carried out receptor imaging in the brain by a different but invasive approach called autoradiography. He brought that skill to the PET team.

[2]   For review, see Volkow N. et al. "Imaging dopamine's role in drug abuse and addiction." *Neuropharmacol,* 56 (Suppl) 1:3–8, 2009.

[3]   Receptor autoradiography is a procedure that visualizes drug receptors in slices of brain with the microscope. Being able to see receptors and where they are is an immense help in determining what drugs might be doing in the brain and how the brain adjusts to repeated drug taking.

Human interest stories about scientists can be fascinating. James Watson's "Double Helix" was quite popular. Sometimes scientists, being human, forget who did what and how things were done. In a book called *Molecules of Emotion* (New York: Scribner, 1997), the author confuses the order in which things were done and who did the developmental work in receptor autoradiography. In fact, the home department of the senior developer was not even correct in the book. The autoradiographic approach to localizing receptors in brain was done by the author (M. Kuhar), a collaborator (H. Yamamura), and a graduate student (W.S. Young III) who are the authors of the relevant papers. Existing notebooks, photography logs, publications, and written recollections of those involved solidly support this. The appropriate publications are Kuhar, M.J. and H.I. Yamamura. "Light Autoradiographic Localization of Cholinergic Muscarinic Receptors in Rat Brain by Specific Binding of a Potent Antagonist." *Nature,* 253: 560–561, 1975. Young, W.S. and M.J. Kuhar. "Autoradiographic Localization of Benzodiazepine Receptors in the Brain of Humans and Animals." *Nature,* 280: 393–395 1979. Young, W.S., III, and M.J. Kuhar. "A New Method for Receptor Autoradiography: [3H]Opioid Receptors in Rat Brain." *Brain Research,* 179: 255–273, 1979. Collaborations with others began after the details were worked out by this initial group.

4　Kuhar, M.J. "Measuring Levels of Proteins by Various Technologies: Can We Learn More by Measuring Turnover?" *Biochem Pharmacol*, 79:665–668, 2010.

5　Nader M. et al. "PET Imaging of Dopamine D2 Receptors During Chronic Cocaine Self-Administration in Monkeys." *Nature Neurosci*, 9:1050–1056, 2006.

8

Could I Become an Addict?

"Why me, Doc? Why am I the one hooked on drugs in my family? Why do I have all this trouble? Maybe I'm a bad seed..." Conversations like this can be common between drug users and their doctors. Understanding why someone is a drug user is a complex and important problem.

"Vulnerability"—Who Will Take Drugs?

Drug users are a diverse population of individuals, and drug abuse, in general, is a complex process. But, key questions are the following: What traits or characteristics do drug users share? Can we identify groups or individuals that will become addicts or are in danger of becoming addicts? It would be a great thing if we could, because then we could target these people for prevention and treatment. Targeting just this group would likely save lots of money and possibly be more effective because the efforts would be focused rather than broadly aimed and widespread.

It turns out that we have studied drug users and addicts and have identified factors that are more common among them than among the general population. These factors contribute to the vulnerability to becoming a drug user. At the outset of this discussion, we can say that we don't know enough about vulnerability to precisely predict who will become an addict and who won't. There is no mathematical equation that we can use! Rather, vulnerability studies provide more of a *probability* of becoming a drug user. In general, the more

vulnerability factors that a person possesses, the greater the likelihood that he or she will become an addict—but again, there is no
certainty. Nonetheless, someone with vulnerability factors should be
interested in this topic in order to assess what he or she needs to do to
avoid becoming involved with drugs. It can be scary for many to face
this, but understanding vulnerability is one of the best ways to prevent drug use and become a healthier person in general.

Factors Creating Vulnerability

There are a large number of factors that contribute to vulnerability
(see Figure 8-1), and some of the most critical ones are discussed
here. The first ones are the biological factors, which help us address a
key issue: Is it in my genes? If so, will I become a drug user no matter
what I do?

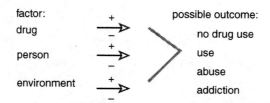

Figure 8-1   Overall vulnerability to drug use comes from several interacting
factors. Let's consider three factors in becoming a drug abuser. First, there is
the drug, which might or might not be addicting (hence the + or –), but for our
discussion it is an addicting substance. Then there is the person who has a
genetic basis that might or might not (hence the + and –) support drug taking.
Lastly, there is the complexity of the environment, in which there might be
drugs and various factors that might or might not support drug taking. Thus,
the overall vulnerability can be high or low depending on each factor and how
they add up or interact. On the right, the range of possible outcomes are
listed. Treatment should address all of the factors. (Adapted from "Figure 1"
from O'Brien, CP. Review: Evidence-Based Treatments of Addiction. "Philos
Trans R Soc Lond." B Biol Sci. 363(1507):3277–86, Oct 12, 2008, with permission.)

Our Genes and Proteins

After a person's first exposure to a drug, his or her biological makeup plays a major role in determining whether he or she will become a drug abuser. Because a person's biological makeup is determined by genes, there has been a focus of research on genes that are involved in drug abuse. Studies of genes have developed exponentially over the last couple of decades. Many of these studies rely on mutations that we carry and they can be identified by amazing, high-throughput technologies.

Tracking Genes

Understanding genes, their mutations, and how they are used gives us an appreciation of how genetic studies are carried out in addiction and even in other diseases.

Imagine your ancestors, many, many generations ago. You have many men and women in your ancestral tree and the further you go back in time, the more there are. Over time, mutations occur in various genes, and if they are not fatal, then they are passed on from generation to generation. Some of the mutations might be small without any functional effect, or some might have an effect that reduces function but is not fatal. The mutations that are not fatal are passed down and—here is the critical part— they can be detected as markers of heredity. In other words, if a group of people have the same mutation that is not found throughout the population, then chances are that the members of the group share a common ancestor. Because they share the same mutation, they also share and express the effects of that mutation, which, for example, might be a slightly increased liking (or vulnerability) for certain kinds of drugs.

The following schematic shows DNA in the well-known shape of a double helix.

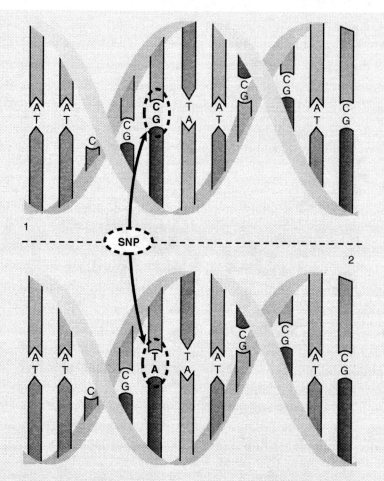

The genetic markers that are used in studies of heritability are often single nucleotide polymorphisms (SNPs). Genes consist of strings of molecular units called nucleotides. Nucleotides come in four varieties, which differ from each other only in the sub-units known as bases. Each nucleotide is named after its base: adenine (A), thymine (T), cytosine (C), or guanine (G). At many locations in the human genome, the nucleotide string that makes up a particular gene is identical in everyone. That is, if you start at one end of the gene and count off the nucleotides in order along one of the two DNA strands, the result is the same—for example, AAGGGATCCAC. At certain places along the string, however, *some people have one nucleotide and others have a different one*—for example, AAGGAATCCAC, instead of the more common sequence. Such a variation is a SNP (also see the next sidebar "Genome-Wide Association Studies [GWAS]"). (Adapted from http://en.wikipedia.org/wiki/File:Dna-SNP.svg, accessed on November 23, 2010.)

A powerful study was carried out by Dr. George Uhl and his colleagues at the National Institute on Drug Abuse. They used an approach called *genome-wide association studies* (see the next sidebar "Genome-Wide Association Studies [GWAS]"), where the genes in drug users are compared to those in non-drug users (or in low-level drug users). After examining the genes in these populations, they found that 89 genes were associated with drug use. Uhl explained further that "unlike cystic fibrosis which is caused by a single (defective) gene, in addiction and a number of complex disorders, many different genes must act together with environmental factors to create the illness. No single gene is likely to have a large effect by itself; it's the combination of effects that produce ... the problem."[1] Many of these 89 genes were known to be associated with memory formation, receptors, and adherence of neurons to each other. It makes sense that those kinds of genes would be involved in drug dependence, which produces biochemical and functional changes in the brain.

Genome-Wide Association Studies (GWAS)

GWAS is a powerful way to identify genes that are associated with traits or diseases. It depends on having a test population that has the trait of interest (such as drug taking) and a control population that does not have the trait. Then, all the genes in all of the subjects are characterized and the occurrence of genetic markers in the populations are compared.

The genetic markers that are used are SNPs (see previous sidebar, "Tracking Genes").

Studies can look at hundreds of thousands of SNPs that occur among our approximately 30,000 genes by relatively rapid, computerized techniques.

The variations (SNPs) might or might not make a difference in the way a gene functions. (For example, two similar model cars but with different color are like SNPs where there is no difference in function. But the same model cars with very different sized engines might function differently.) So, SNPs don't have to be functionally powerful; but they are good markers for studying the heritability of specific genes. Scientists can take advantage of the SNP variations to discover associations between genes and critical traits, such as vulnerability to drug addiction. For example, if a certain SNP occurs more often in drug abusers than in non-drug abusers, then the gene that contains the SNP is said to be associated with, and possibly partly causing, drug addiction. (Adapted from "New Techniques Link 89 genes to Drug Dependence," *NIDA Notes*, Vol. 22, September 2008.)

There have been interesting new discoveries about the genes related to smoking and the vulnerability for nicotine addiction. As noted, nicotine works in the brain by stimulating receptors for acetylcholine, which are referred to as nicotinic cholinergic receptors. Nicotinic receptors are made up of five separate proteins that bundle together to form a functioning receptor. These proteins, or subunits, have been identified and studied (see Figure 8-2); when combined, they create the various subtypes of nicotinic receptors. Surprisingly, there are more than five subunits, but only five are used in any given receptor. When the different nicotinic receptors have different subunits, they might function differently, and different people inherit different subunits from their parents.

Now here's the relevant part. Studies have linked various subunits to aspects of smoking (see the following sidebar). It is this kind of research that leads to real understandings of the molecules of addiction—and ultimately to improve medications for such addicts. Again, the brain is complex, and having a "bad" subtype does not mean that someone will, without question, have the addiction. But, he or she will have an increased overall vulnerability.

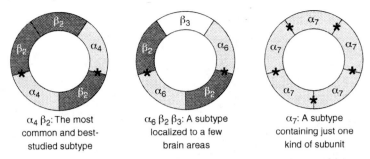

$\alpha_4\,\beta_2$: The most common and best-studied subtype

$\alpha_6\,\beta_2\,\beta_3$: A subtype localized to a few brain areas

α_7: A subtype containing just one kind of subunit

Figure 8-2　Nicotine acts at receptors for the neurotransmitter acetylcholine. These receptors, which are ion-gated receptors, are shown from a more sideways perspective in Figure 4-2, but from a more top-down view in this figure. These nicotinic cholinergic receptors are composed of five subunit proteins that bundle together to form a circle around a central pore. When acetylcholine or nicotine binds to the receptor proteins (at the places marked with an asterisk), ions (electrical charges) migrate through the pore into the post-synaptic neuron. The receptors can be composed of a variety of different subunits to produce a variety of subtypes of nicotinic receptors. Some of these subtypes are shown in the figure. Receptors comprised of different subtypes might function differently and confer different levels of vulnerability to smoking. (From NIDA Notes, "Studies Link Family of Genes to Nicotine Addiction," Vol. 22, December 2009.)

Aspect of Smoking	Gene Subunit
Dizziness from first cigarette	$\beta3$
Pleasure from initial cigarette	$\alpha5$
Increased risk of dependence among early smokers	$\alpha5$
Lung cancer and peripheral arterial disease	$\alpha3$

Genetic studies have become amazingly sophisticated, and it is a triumph that many different receptor subunits have been related to aspects of smoking. This sidebar summarizes some of the work in this area relating smoking to nicotinic receptor subunits. Findings such as these can guide our efforts in the search for new medications, and they offer hope that someday we will understand enough about drug addiction that we can develop better medications for treating drug users. (Adapted from NIDA Notes, "Studies Link Family of Genes to Nicotine Addiction," Vol. 22, December 2009.)

This information tells us that the influence of our genes on drug taking varies from person to person, and that each person has a different level of biological vulnerability. Most people exposed to addicting drugs do not become addicts. Data shows that the likelihood of addiction is partly due to hereditary factors—our genes. But environmental factors (for example, the availability of drugs, high stress, emotional problems, and peer pressure to use drugs) are essential. Although genetics might account for as much as 20–40 percent of our vulnerability,[2] it isn't correct to blame just our genetics for our level of drug use.

Psychological Problems

Drug use in individuals is often associated with a variety of emotional problems such as depression, anxiety, schizophrenia, post-traumatic stress disorder (PTSD), and other complicated problems referred to as antisocial personality disorders and conduct disorders. In one study, between 21 and 32 percent of nicotine-dependent subjects had an additional mental health diagnosis. Although this made up only 7.1 percent of the population, they consumed more than 34 percent of all the cigarettes in the U.S.[3]

Some of these mental health disorders might either be caused by, or exist independently of, substance use. In any case, they can facilitate drug use—a justification for treating both problems when an individual suffers from both drug use and a mental health disorder. Sometimes, withdrawal or cessation of drug use can precipitate problems such as anxiety; in this instance, treating the mental problem can make drug addiction treatment more successful. Related to this, it has been suggested that at least some drug addicts begin using drugs to self-medicate and treat problems such as anxiety. This means that if you use addicting drugs, you might have a mental health problem in addition to the use of drugs. If you do, then dealing with that will reduce your vulnerability to drug taking. Mental problems can weaken our resolve to deal with other issues (such as drug use) in our lives. They can distract and exhaust us, and possibly lead to self-medicating, which might be problematic. Although treating our ills is, of course, important, a doctor's involvement is often needed, particularly when abusable drugs are involved.

Temperament and Personality Traits

Many studies show a correlation between personal temperament and drug use. For example, impulsivity, physical activity level, having difficulty sitting still, and the tendency to become emotionally upset have been correlated with higher drug use. On the other hand, having a more positive mood and a desire to be around people have been *negatively* correlated with drug use. Often, personality traits in *adolescence* correlate with higher drug use as *adults*. This is clearly an important topic and an active area of research.

Availability of Drugs

Availability of drugs is obviously a major factor in becoming a drug user. If drugs were not available, then there would be no users. But, drugs are available in many places, and staying away from drugs is essential for recovering addicts (and everyone else, of course). For example, Alcoholics Anonymous focuses on staying away from alcohol and provides a support system for doing so. Availability can have a marked and destructive effect on an entire community.

Kids, Teenagers, and Adults

Adolescents are a special case. Being exposed to drug use or participating in drug use at an early age has an impact on drug use later in life. Figure 8-3 shows that there is a relationship between the age at which drugs are first used and the likelihood that the same person will become drug dependent at some later time in his or her life.

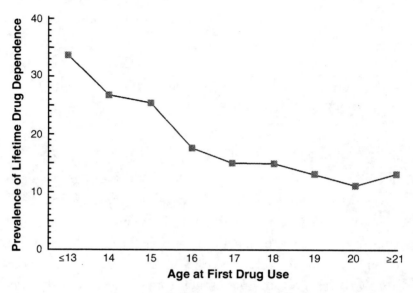

Figure 8-3   Adolescent drug use increases the likelihood of drug dependence later in life. (Reprinted from *Journal of Substance Abuse*, Vol. 10, Bridget F. Grant and Deborah A. Dawson, "Age of onset of drug use and its association with DSM-IV drug abuse and dependence: Results from the national longitudinal alcohol epidemiological survey," pp. 163-173, Copyright (1998), with permission from Elsevier.)

The data shows that when drugs are used before about 17 years of age, the likelihood of dependence at some time later in life rises dramatically.

There is plenty of physiologic evidence that the adolescent brain can be more responsive to drugs than adult brains. For example, dopamine neurons (which many drugs affect) in the adolescent rat are more sensitive to stimulation than those in adult rats (see Figure 8-4). The young neurons are different; their response to a particular stimulus is greater than that of an older neuron.

This is definitely a message for parents and communities, and it makes young people an important target for prevention efforts.

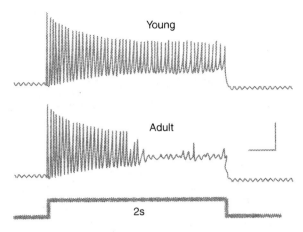

Figure 8-4   Dopamine neurons in the Ventral Tegmental Area (VTA) in young mice are more responsive than those in adult mice. The dopamine neurons in the VTA, in a slice of mouse brain, were stimulated for 2 seconds (shown by elevated line on bottom trace) and the elicited action potentials were recorded. An individual action potential is shown as an upward line rising sharply from the baseline. There are many more action potentials in young neurons than in adult neurons. Young dopamine neurons are capable of responding more than adult neurons to the same stimulus. The VTA is a region containing dopamine cell bodies that is relevant to developing addiction. (Reprinted from *Biochemical Pharmacology*, Vol. 78, Andon N. Placzek, Tao A. Zhang, and John A. Dani, "Age dependent nicotinic influences over dopamine neuron synaptic plasticity," pp. 686-692, Copyright (2009), with permission from Elsevier.)

Drugs Impair Our Judgment and Perpetuate Drug Use

In many ways, drug abusers are among the least capable of stopping drug use. As they become intoxicated, their normal, cognitive and self-regulating abilities become compromised. For example, as they become drunk on alcohol, it becomes more difficult to stop drinking for several reasons. One reason is that the person is less aware of what he or she is doing, and the cognitive function, which is needed to help assess the situation, is impaired. Drug use can impair the function of brain regions such as the orbitofrontal cortex and anterior cingulate gyrus that are involved in judgment, decision making, and inhibition of unwanted activities like drug taking. These impairments contribute to a lack of control, compulsive drug taking, and a general impairment of judgment that favors relapse to drug use. This was shown by

Dr. Edythe London and colleagues and others in a gambling task; drug abusers were much more likely to make bad decisions that resulted in long-term losses.[4] Taking drugs can make things worse and result in a nasty, downward spiral.

What About Me?

What if you are right now saying, "Oh my gosh, I have a lot of those factors for vulnerability?" Or, what if you know somebody important to you who seems to be loaded with vulnerability? Or maybe some friends are trying to stop drinking but have no idea about these factors and what they mean for them. Well, now is the time to pay attention and listen up.

These are "risk" factors, and risk is not certainty. Risk is about an increased likelihood. Nevertheless, thinking about risk factors can be helpful. If certain factors apply to someone, then he or she has to work extra hard in controlling these and other factors. For example, someone who has a strong family history of drug dependence might have a hereditary vulnerability that, of course, can't be avoided. However, this just means that the person would have to work at other factors like avoiding places where drugs are available, avoiding friends who use, and seeking positive support from counselors, clergy, friends, and family members. The more risk factors that one has, the more vulnerable he or she is. So, working at controlling the risk factors that one can influence is important. Life is short, and strengthening positive and healthy habits will mean a lot. When in risky situations, being aware of the danger of drugs and being prepared to say no to drugs are crucial to combating risk factors.

The Rider and His Elephant

Here is an interesting story. Jonathan Haidt tells us in his book[5] of the metaphorical concept of the "elephant and the rider" to describe our control of emotional drives and actions. Both the elephant and rider are found in each of us and represent different aspects of our psyche. The rider is intelligent with a grip on the reigns that guides the elephant in its tasks (or through life). The rider can see the overall task, is responsible for it, and has the judgment and skills to deal with it. The rider is associated with our conscience, our conscious and controlled thinking, and planning for the future. Perhaps the rider is like Freud's super ego and ego.

The elephant on the other hand, is the rest of our psyche; it includes fears, emotions, intuitions, and visceral reactions. It contains the reward and reinforcement centers in our brains, and embodies the powerful drives that lurk in the old parts of our brain that have helped our species survive. Like the rider, the elephant has knowledge, but of a different kind. It is more like Freud's id or primitive drives. In our psyche, the elephant represents drives and appetites that are perhaps more subconscious than conscious.

When a skilled rider teams with a strong elephant, both can do well and accomplish much. However—and here is the point—the elephant within us, being so big and powerful in comparison to the rider within us, will do whatever it wants or feels it must under certain circumstances. If the elephant is suddenly attacked by a hungry tiger, it will react powerfully and pay no attention to the rider no matter how knowledgeable the rider is about fighting tigers. When a stimulus strikes the elephant as overwhelmingly dangerous, reflexive drives take over and the rational thinker is left struggling for control. The rider is vulnerable to losing control of the elephant.

This is one way we can think of drug addiction or abuse. Drugs are seen by both the rider and the elephant within us, and the question is, who will control our actions? If our appetites for drugs dominate, the elephant might take over. The primitive drives and appetites that have ensured the survival of our species are very strong. If the sensible rider has an influence over the elephant and can guide its actions, we might avoid drugs. Whether we take drugs or not depends on our overall vulnerability (how much the elephant wants it versus how skilled and determined the rider is to avoid it). A major factor is how well the rider has been trained, and on how well the rider has trained the elephant within. Responding to crises can be prepared for, at least to some degree.

What about the responsibility of the rider for the elephant? We all know that we cannot totally give up responsibility for control of our elephant. If we take drugs and have an accident, then we are responsible. If we take illegal drugs and have to face the law, it is our fault. It is clear that we must take responsibility to maintain law and society. But perhaps there are some circumstances—the equivalent of the appearance of a hungry tiger—where absolute control by the rider is diminished and his responsibility is reduced. Dealing with these difficult circumstances requires wisdom and often help.

Summary

The major message of this chapter is that individuals might have to work hard to take care of themselves. If they have risk factors for becoming a drug user, then they need to pay attention to them. If there are some that they can't avoid, like genetic factors or drugs in the environment, then they have to work doubly hard at controlling the risk factors that they can. If drugs are being sold or are available, then avoiding those places and people and practicing the ability to say no is important. A conference with a physician or another professional would be helpful.

Endnotes

[1]   From *NIDA Notes*, "New Techniques Link 89 Genes to Drug Dependence." Vol. 22, No.1, September 2008.

[2]   For example, see Table 1.5 in Koob, G.F. and M. Le Moal. *Neurobiology of Addiction*. London: Academic Press, 2006.

3   Grant B.F. et al. "Nicotine Dependence and Psychiatric Disorders in the United States." *Arch Gen Psychiatry*, 61:1107–1115, 2004.

4   Grant S. et al. "Drug Users Show Impaired Performance in a Laboratory Test of Decision Making." *Neuropsychologia*, 38:1180–1187, 2000.

5   Haidt J. *The Happiness Hypothesis*. Cambridge MA: Basic Books, 2006.

9

Stress, Social Status, and Drugs

"After the war, I was a hopeless alcoholic. But with help, I'd been clean for five years—not a sip of alcohol. Life was going so well for me. And then, the recession hit. Traumatic memories of the war returned, I lost my job, and now I'm about to lose my home because I can't pay my mortgage. I'm so stressed out with trying to make ends meet that I've started drinking again."

The more stress we experience, the more likely we are to use drugs. Although stress could have been included in the last chapter on vulnerability, its many interesting aspects warrant that a chapter be devoted to it. A dictionary definition of a stressor is a stimulus that is disturbing, like fear or pain, that alters normal bodily responses. When we are stressed, we are often tense, alert, and prepared to "fight or flee." Stress produces important bodily changes that produce and reinforce the state of alertness and readiness. It is a complex response that has evolved in our bodies because it is important for our survival. However, it is a demanding response, and, as you know, unremitting and chronic stress can be emotionally and physically damaging.

The Body's Response to Stress

How our bodies react to stress has been studied for decades. Stress begins with a stimulus in our environment that we interpret as threatening. It can involve hearing, seeing, touching, or all of these senses. The brain integrates these sensations, and as a result, the amygdala, hypothalamus, and pituitary gland are activated. The amygdala and hypothalamus are parts of the brain associated with fear, stress, and the integration of bodily functions. The pituitary gland, which is controlled by the hypothalamus, is located just beneath the brain and releases hormones needed by the body. As part of the stress response, ACTH, a hormone released from the pituitary gland activates the adrenal glands, which in turn release the stress hormones, epinephrine and cortisol (see Figure 9-1). These hormones act throughout the body to prepare us for responsive action. Epinephrine increases heart rate and blood pressure to help the body meet the new demands. Cortisol increases blood sugar (glucose) to provide more fuel for the energy needed to deal with the stressor, and it does this by promoting the synthesis of glucose and by assisting in the metabolism of fat, protein, and carbohydrates that produce additional glucose. Chronic stress can affect many organ systems and leave us depressed, with aches and pains, nausea, dizziness, rapid heartbeat, and exhaustion. Stress can also suppress our immune system, leaving us with a greater risk for infection.

There are also emotional and mental responses to stress. Normally the frontal cortex, a highly evolved part of the brain, regulates reality testing, guides attention and thought, inhibits inappropriate actions, and regulates emotion. But under stress, other brain regions strongly come into play. The amygdala activates stress pathways in the hypothalamus and brainstem, which results in a loss of prefrontal cortex regulation and disposes us toward habitual responding rather than more cognitively controlled actions. So, stress causes a switch from reflective and modulated responses to emotionally driven reflexive responses.

Stressors can be personal, and what stresses one person might not stress another. There are many kinds of stressors. Environmental stressors include a natural disaster such as an earthquake, the 9/11 terrorist attack, or even such things as uncontrollable loud sounds or bright lights. Life changes such as divorce, job loss, or deaths in the family can be serious stressors. The workplace can be stressful, and this is often related to how much control an employee has over his or her job and its conditions. Also, daily events such as a fender bender, loss of house keys, or theft of a purse or wallet can be very troublesome. Because of the dangers of stress and cumulative layers of stress, we must develop styles and support systems to help us handle it. Stress busters include play and exercise, meditation, improved diet, and medical care.

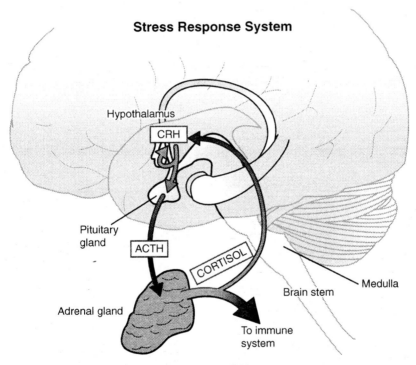

Stress Response System

Figure 9-1   The body's stress response. When someone is stressed, the brain's stress pathways are activated such that the hypothalamus, found in the base of the brain, sends a chemical signal, CRH, to the pituitary gland, which sends another chemical signal, ACTH, to the adrenal glands (found near the kidneys). The adrenals secrete cortisol, which is the well known "stress hormone" into the blood. Cortisol then stimulates a metabolic response and circulates back to the brain to stop or regulate the release of chemicals from the hypothalamus and pituitary. This regulation is important so that this stress response is not a "runaway" process. Many addicts are hypersensitive to stress. (From http://being.publicradio.org/programs/stress/particulars.shtml and Roberto Osti, with permission.)

Stress and Drug Use

Stress can make us start using drugs or cause a relapse to drug use. Dr. Mary Jeanne Kreek of Rockefeller University in New York City has studied stress and relapse among the addicts of New York. She has said, "For six months or so, they (drug addicts) can walk past the street corner where they used to buy drugs and not succumb to their urges. But then all of a sudden they relapse," she says. "When we ask them why they relapse, almost always they tell us something like, 'Well, things weren't going well at my job,' or 'My wife left me.' Sometimes, the problem is as small as 'My public assistance check was delayed,' or 'The traffic was too heavy.'"[1] Many studies have shown that stress can promote relapse to drug use, even after long periods of abstinence. It can also worsen drug use in an active user and initiate or worsen other psychiatric disorders such as anxiety and depression, which can make drug use worse. Addicts are more susceptible to stress and are often already stressed. For example, withdrawal, or doing the work of avoiding drugs, can be stressful activities, and adding more stress can create a stress overload, resulting in relapse to drug taking. The act of just taking a drug can also be stressful.

Individuals suffering from post-traumatic stress disorder (PTSD) are of concern. They are people such as war veterans who re-live and re-experience horrible battle situations so vividly that they seem real. It's a stress that occurs after the original trauma actually happened, but is so intense that it requires treatment. Of course, stress is subjective and PTSD does not have to come from wartime experiences. It can come from accidents, crimes, or other very bad experiences. PTSD sufferers are at greater risk for drug use as well.

Treating stress is important, but because of the danger of relapse, it is probably more important in a drug user.[2] However, medical supervision and much care are needed because some of the medications for treating stress and anxiety are themselves addicting.

Although stress is a risk factor for drug use, it is fortunate that it can be worked with, treated, and at least partially controlled.

Early Life Stress

A most amazing finding has been that stress in early life seems to change us—for the rest of our lives! This story began when scientists found an association between adverse events in early life, nicotine dependence in adults, and a strong relationship between household dysfunction when growing up and drug use as an adult. A variety of animal studies, by Drs. Michael Meaney, Darlene Francis, Paul Plotsky, and others, were carried out that supported these findings.

The author and his laboratory colleagues carried out the following experiment. Litters of newborn rat pups were divided into groups. Although there were several groups, we need to examine only two to make the point. One group of new born rats was separated from their mothers (referred to as dams) for 15 minutes a day (referred to as MS15), every day, during the first two weeks of life. A second group was separated from the dams for 3 hours every day (referred to as MS180) during the first two weeks of life. A separation of 15 minutes is not considered stressful, presumably because in nature, the mother must leave the nest for short periods to obtain food, and perhaps offspring are "programmed" to tolerate short separations. But a 3-hour separation is considered to be stressful for the pups. After the two weeks when the daily separations were carried out, all groups of pups were then placed with their mothers and raised just like all of the other animals in the vivarium until they were adults. There were no more separations until the pups were routinely weaned from their dams. When the pups were adults, they were tested to see how and if they would self-administer alcohol. The more stressed group (MS180) showed a greater preference for and a greater intake of alcohol than the normal (MS15) group (see Figure 9-2). The same was found true for cocaine. A similar experiment was carried out by Dr. T.A. Kosten and coworkers, who separated pups from the dams for one hour. The separated animals, when they were adults, were more sensitive to cocaine in that they recognized lower doses of cocaine and self-administered it (see Figure 9-3). It is amazing that stressful experiences around the time of birth can influence drug taking much later in life when the animals are adults.

Ethanol Preference

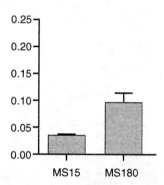

Figure 9-2   Early life stress affects alcohol intake when we are adults. Rat pups were separated from their mothers (dams) for either 15 minutes (MS15) or 180 minutes (MS180) everyday for two weeks right after birth. After these two weeks of daily separation, they were then treated like all other rats in the facility. But, when they became adults, they were tested for their inclination to drink alcohol. Although a 15-minute separation is not considered very stressful because dams in the wild must leave their pups for short times to get food, a 180-minute separation is considered stressful. As adults, the MS180 (more stressed) group had a greater preference for, and a greater intake of, alcohol than the MS15 (less stressed) group. This suggests that early life stressors can change our sensitivities to drugs and our behaviors for the rest of our lives! (With kind permission from Springer Science+Business Media: *Psychopharmacology*, "Effects of early maternal separation on ethanol intake, GABA receptors and metabolizing enzymes in adult rats," Vol. 181 (2005) 11, Jaworski, JN, Francis, DD, Brommer, CL, Morgan, ET, and Kuhar, MJ, Figure 1.)

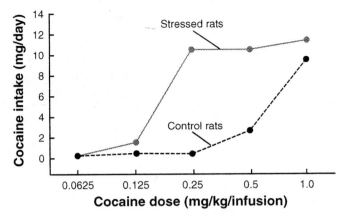

Figure 9-3 Stressed rats take more cocaine. A group of rats were stressed just after birth by removing them from their mother for just one hour per day for eight days. After the eight days of daily, brief stress, the rat pups were allowed to grow up like all other unstressed, normal rats in all other normal litters. As adults, the rats that were stressed as pups recognized cocaine at lower doses, and more readily self-administered cocaine! This shows that stresses around the time of birth can have effects that extend to adulthood, and that stressors in the perinatal period can result in greater drug taking as adults. (Reprinted from *Brain Research*, Vol. 875, Therese A. Kosten, Mindy J. D. Miserendino, and Priscilla Kehoe, "Enhanced acquisition of cocaine self-administration in adult rats with neonatal isolation stress experience," pp. 44-50, Copyright [2000], with permission from Elsevier.)

Although only part of the early life stress story has been described here, many studies from other laboratories support these findings. Surprisingly, these findings are not always well appreciated. Even pharmacology textbooks do not describe how early life factors can alter the response to drugs in adulthood. It is remarkable how our childhood environment can shape a variety of behavior when we are adults. We can guess that the early life stressors cause changes in gene expression that are maintained throughout life by epigenetic mechanisms, which are described in Chapter 5, "The Dark Side Develops!"

Social Rank Affects Cocaine Intake!

Low social status is often characterized by violence, financial problems, poor health, shame and defeat, feelings of inferiority and insecurity, and anxiety and depression. All of these are stressors, and drug use can be higher in this population. The importance of social status has been neatly demonstrated in well designed studies with animals. For example, Drs. M. Nader, D. Morgan, K. Grant, and others performed experiments showing that social rank in a group of monkeys can affect the dopamine system in the brain, and consequently, the amount of cocaine that is self-administered. In one study, monkeys (20 cynomologus macaques) were housed individually for one and a half years, and their D2 dopamine receptor levels were measured by PET scans. D2 dopamine receptors, critical parts of the dopamine system, were measured because they have been associated with addictive behavior as described in Chapter 4, "The ABCs of Drug Action in the Brain," and Chapter 7, "The Brain Is Changed— For a Long Time!" Critical parts of their dopamine systems, the receptors, were measured when they were housed alone. Then, the animals were formed into five groups of four animals each, and the animals in each social group lived together for several months. During that time, the animals in the groups formed social hierarchies; dominant and subordinate monkeys emerged, as expected. The dominant monkeys were groomed more often by the others, were more aggressive, and were submitted to more often than the others. Their D2 receptor levels were again measured by PET scans, and their cocaine self-administration behavior was also measured.

The results were remarkable! The levels of D2 dopamine receptors increased in the brains of the animals that became dominant, but were unchanged in the subordinate animals! There was a relationship between social status and D2 dopamine receptor levels, and when the levels were found to be higher, the social status was higher (see Table 9-1). Because of the earlier discussion (in Chapter 7) that low D2 levels relate to greater drug taking, the drug intake of dominant animals was examined and compared to that of the subordinate animals. Low and behold, the dominant animals, the ones with the higher D2 receptor levels, took less cocaine than the subordinate animals.

TABLE 9–1   Effect of Changing from Individual to Social Housing, and the Effect of Establishing a Social Hierarchy

Animals Who Became:	Changes in D2 Dompamine Receptors	Effect on Drug Taking
Most dominant	22% increase	Higher ranks took less cocaine.
Most submissive	No siginificant change	Lower ranks took more cocaine.

Animals were individually housed and their levels of D2 receptors were measured by PET scans. Then they were put into social groups, hierarchies were established, and their receptors levels were measured again. The animals that became most dominant had increases in their receptor levels, whereas the submissive ones didn't. Also, the most dominant animals self-administered less cocaine than the submissive ones. (Summarized from D. Morgan et al. "Social Dominance in Monkeys: Dopamine D2 Receptors and Cocaine Self-Administration." *Nature Neuroscience*, 5:169-174, 2002.)

Placing the previously isolated animals in a social situation, where some become dominant, changed the biochemistry of the brains of the dominant ones and made them less vulnerable to cocaine, in just several months. Our social situations, or social rank if you will, can influence our brains and our vulnerability to take drugs, and presumably our vulnerability to other problems as well. This has many implications and questions for our lives. What is it in our brains, personality, or environment that determines our drive for dominance (or submission), and how does this impact our brain so that crucial changes occur in the brain? We can attempt a reasonable answer for the second question. Sensory input, like stress, activates the neurotransmitter systems in the brain, and, as described in Chapter 4, activation of neurotransmitter pathways can produce alterations (or plasticities) in these pathways. One kind of alteration is a change in levels of receptors or other components of the neurotransmission process.

Social Defeat!

We all experience what could be called "social defeats" in our lives. They might include being turned down when you ask someone to dance, being ridiculed publicly, or being excluded from a social group that is important to you. Moreover, you can become sensitized to it such that you feel defeated more easily when repeatedly confronted by the same defeating situation. Depending on exactly what the defeat is and depending on your social situation, needs, maturity, and resilience, you might be significantly affected by it. However, everyone has experienced situations of social defeat that can be quite devastating, and it is understandable that some turn to drugs to deal with the emotional pain. This has been studied in animals. For example, placing two male rats together under certain conditions results in one animal becoming subordinate or defeated. He might lie on his back and defer to the more dominant animal. In general, socially defeated animals behave differently. They explore less and are less active, they forage and eat less, and they engage in reproductive behavior less often. And here is the interesting part. The defeated animals also take some drugs such as cocaine more readily. Specifically, some experiments show that defeated animals learn to take cocaine faster than nondefeated animals.[3] A possible interpretation of this is that defeated animals (and humans too) are in pain and want drugs more. Social defeat, whatever that means for each of us, can promote drug use.

Enriched Environments: The Other Side of the Coin

Stressful environments increase the vulnerability to use drugs. But what about pleasant or enriching environments? Do they do the opposite? There *is* strong evidence that they, in fact, will do the opposite.

Normally, laboratory rodents like mice or rats are housed under what are called standard conditions, which are adequately sized cages with bedding, food, and water. Enriched environments include larger cages with running wheels, small houses, and four or five colorful toys of various shapes that are changed weekly. Animals stay in these enriched environments for perhaps 30 days before testing, and their behavior is compared to animals that stayed in standard housing.

Many laboratories have reported that environmental enrichment reduces cocaine seeking and stress-induced drug taking. In animals already experienced with cocaine (they have learned to self-administer it), environmental enrichment can reduce or even eliminate some addiction-related behaviors. Similar results have been found with other drugs such as heroin. When gene expression was examined in enriched animals (without drugs), many changes were found. Genes for proteins involved in synaptic transmission, protein production, cell structure, and metabolism were affected. These changes in the brain undoubtedly underlie the behavioral changes brought about by environmental enrichment. This work suggests that positive life conditions can change your brain chemistry and can even help addicts stay away from drugs. It is further suggested that positive environments can improve our lives in many, perhaps unexpected, ways. The important message here is that, like drugs, environments and behaviors change the brain. Because of this, they have the potential to serve as antidotes for drug addiction.

Summary

Stress in our lives is unavoidable, and dealing with it remains a problem for many people. We read self-help books, meditate, join various kinds of anti-stress groups and practices, complain, and suffer its effects. It might drive us to eat more for comfort, withdraw socially, or seek help from counselors. Even relatively common stressors such as overbearing bosses, traffic congestion, and so on, can promote drug taking. There is also early life stress that seems to predispose us to drug taking when we are adults, many months and years after the original stressor. Social rank and social defeat can also drive drug use. Thus, the effects of stressors are substantial and enduring, and stress is clearly a risk factor for drug use and relapse to drug use. Fortunately, this risk factor can, at least to some degree, be controlled. Improved, positive environments seem to reduce vulnerability to drug seeking and relapse. Stress is something we need to learn to handle to reduce destructive consequences.

Endnotes

[1] Taken from *NIDA Notes*, Vol 14, April 1999.

[2] The National Institute on Drug Abuse has made a special point about the importance of stress in addiction. See *NIDA Notes*, "NIDA Community Drug Alert Bulletin—Stress & Substance Abuse," February 2006.

[3] For example, see Tidey J.W., Miczek K.A. "Acquisition of cocaine self-administration after social stress: role of accumbens dopamine." *Psychopharmacology (Berl)*, Apr;130(3):203-12, 1997.

10

Gambling, Sex, and Food

As he drove past the casino, he could see the marquee, the valet parking stand...and the feelings started up again. He felt the thrill of placing a bet, of winning a pot. He felt energy, and his mind went faster. He wanted to be there, and he could feel the very cards in his hands...As he drove farther and the casino was left far behind, he mumbled, "Staying away is getting a little easier, but it's far from easy."

Can we be addicted to something besides drugs? Maybe we can. Consider the broad definition of addiction, which is a search for, or a preoccupation with something, that ends up being distressing or destructive to you, and you can't easily stop.[1] In recent years, there have been more and more studies of various forms of behavioral addiction such as excessive gambling, eating, and sexual activity. The different kinds of addictions have many things in common. First of all, the behavior takes up a lot of time and effort, and it gradually gets out of control such that attempts at stopping or controlling it are unsuccessful. These activities might result in conflicts with teachers, friends, and family members. It might affect the mood and health of the person, and impact the individual's finances, education, or work. Sound familiar?

Excessive or pathological gambling can be considered as "addictive" in several ways. There are powerful rewards—money and the thrill of winning. The problem is that you need time and money to gamble, and this can obviously be a problem when a gambler is overextended and losing. It is sometimes regarded as an impulse control problem. Many people stay away from gambling, saying that they don't trust themselves. Like drug use, pathological gambling has been with us throughout history (see "Gambling Addiction Is Ancient and Enduring"), and it is not a passing fad. When a behavior is found over many generations and in many cultures, it seems that it is part of our human inclinations.

Gambling Addiction Is Ancient and Enduring

The loss of control that some experience when gambling was described thousands of years ago in Indian Sanskrit. In the following story, Yudhishtira cannot stop even though he loses all his possessions, and then he even offers his wife as a bet.

"Have you come to play dice," demanded Duryodhana.

"A king may not lawfully refuse a challenge from another king," said Lord Dharma (Yudhishtira).

"I challenge you," said Duryodhana.

"I will play."

"I will offer this magnificent golden chain as my stake."

Yudhishtira lost, of course. The dice they played was not our modern game of pure chance, but a game that involved number skills and quick hands, and Sakuni (Duryodhana's ally) was an expert. And he cheated. Probably. It's impossible to know for sure that he cheated, and it is really beside the point anyway. Yudhishtira lost everything—his palaces and lands and herds, his chariots and his servants, the very clothes on his back.

Sakuni said, "Do you want to play again?"

"What is left?" said Yudhishtira, wearily.

"Your wife."

"Play."

(From Mahabharata's "The Game of Dice," accessed at http://www.wmblake.com/stories/mahabharata/dicing.htm, on April 19, 2011. The Mahabharata is a major Sanskrit epic of ancient India.)

There have been many studies on gambling.[2] Studies of twins suggest that there is a genetic factor in becoming a gambler. If one member of a twin pair is a gambler, the other member is more likely to be a gambler than an unrelated person. Also, the dopamine system has been associated with gambling. Just as we have described a dysfunction of the frontal cortex in drug users, a similar problem has been found in gamblers who were studied using a card game. Gambling has been correlated with drug use suggesting a common connection or vulnerability of the two. Several imaging studies have shown that pathological gambling involves the same areas of the brain as substance abuse (for example, see Figure 10-1). This further implies that both gambling and substance abuse use the same neuronal circuits, such as the dopamine-containing mesolimbic circuit, which is so critical in drug abuse.

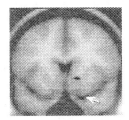

Figure 10-1   Gambling activates the same brain regions as drugs. Subjects participating in the study watched a game where they could either win or lose money. Activations (small darkened areas) were found in the Nucleus accumbens (near arrow tips), a region involved in drug abuse. The two images are at slightly different levels where the one on the right is more forward (towards the forehead). (Reprinted from Neuron, 30, Hans C. Breiter, Itzhak Aharon, Daniel Kahneman, Anders Dale, and Peter Shizgal, Functional Imaging of Neural Responses to Expectancy and Experience of Monetary Gains and Losses, 619-639, Copyright [2001], with permission from Elsevier.)

Treatment for pathological gambling has been mainly behavioral, involving counseling, family therapy, twelve-step programs (Gamblers Anonymous), and the like. The use of medications has not yet been well studied but it is getting attention. There are also treatment centers for gamblers, although their number is very small compared to the centers for treating substance abuse. Overall, pathological gambling seems to be similar to drug addiction, and it will undoubtedly benefit from the extensive work done for drug addiction. But, more studies specific to gambling need to be carried out.

Sexual Addiction

There is some controversy about whether or not sexual "addiction" really exists.[3] But again, one could look at the main criteria for addiction and see that certain extremes of sexual behavior are similar. Sue Williams Silverman, a writer, speaker, and teacher at the Vermont College of Fine Arts, has written *Love Sick: One Woman's Journey Through Sexual Addiction* (W.W. Norton and Co., 2001) that describes her problem and her treatment. She says that she was addicted not only to sex but also to danger, and an addiction to drugs seems similar to her descriptions. She tells of her obsessions, fantasies, and her experiences with strangers, friends, and her father. Her emotional struggle is told with an engaging clarity that makes the reader both wince and struggle with her. Whether or not experts can agree on the term "addiction," sex is a behavior that can be taken to extremes and create problems in our lives.

Although it does mention various sexual disorders, the *DSM-IV TR*, the latest official diagnostic manual of the American Psychiatric Association, does not list the disorder "Sexual Addiction." It doesn't list gambling as an addiction either, but it describes pathological gambling. The *DSM-IV TR* has been put together by teams of thoughtful and experienced professionals. It seems likely that behaviors like pathological gambling will be eventually recognized as an addiction. Perhaps a good question is this: Can the addiction model be usefully applied so that treatment of gambling is helped? This is an important and real goal worth pursuing.

Eating Disorder

Many people can't control their eating, and some think of themselves as addicted to food. Margaret Bullitt-Jonas, an Episcopal priest, is someone who has written and lectured about what she refers to as her eating addiction. She describes her feelings of being hopelessly and painfully lost, in danger of losing her health, and having little idea of how it happened or how to get free. She says that food was not delicious nor was eating pleasurable—it was done compulsively. Her father's problem with alcohol stressed the family and played into her own vulnerability. Eventually, she reached bottom emotionally, and her path to health involved meditation, accepting the presence of a higher power, and attending Overeaters Anonymous. Her recovery was holistic—physical, emotional, and spiritual. Her story is one of great courage and commitment.

The media tell us that chocolate, carbohydrates, and fats improve mood, cause craving, and are the objects of binging. Carbohydrates have even been called a new cocaine, because they cause signals in the same parts of the brain that cocaine does. Interestingly, it has been acknowledged that cocaine works through brain pathways involved with natural rewards such as food. Although the assertion that carbs are like cocaine is true, it's not anything we don't already know. Carbs, particularly those made with white flour such as bread and pasta, are sometimes said to be addicting. Signs of this addiction are suggested to be morning cravings, inability to stop eating them, or having withdrawal symptoms consisting of mood swings and irritability when you stop eating them. The potential to develop diabetes and obesity is present as well. Although much of this sounds like addiction, we should be cautious in labeling the behavior.

Pathologic overeating of any food can be like drug seeking and taking, and various laboratory findings support this similarity. For example, Drs. Gene Wang, Nora Volkow, Joanna Fowler, and others showed, in an imaging study, that obese subjects had lower dopamine receptors than non-obese subjects (see Figure 10-2); this is exactly what was found with drug-addicted individuals and implies that excess food can be like a drug (see Chapter 7, "The Brain Is Changed—For a Long Time," Figure 7-2). Also, binge eating has been connected to the genetics of the dopamine transporter in brain (see "The Dopamine

Transporter Is Connected to Binge Eating" in Chapter 6, "Why Are Drugs So Powerful?"). Binging on sugar is also accompanied by an increase of dopamine output in the nucleus accumbens. We can find individuals who crave sweets, who have tried to stop but relapse, and who feel that their food choices are affecting their health, through obesity or diabetes. Taken together, these findings connecting food binging to dopamine, craving, relapsing, and negative impacts on health, suggest that obesity, at least in some forms and conditions, might be like drug addiction.

But, overeating and obesity are also questioned as being properly called addictions even though it appears that many of the characteristics of addiction apply to these disorders. Dr. Bartley Hoebel at Princeton and others have discussed these questions.[4] In a sense, it might not matter, and an important question is, "How can people with these kinds of problems be helped?" It would be interesting if using methods similar to those from the drug abuse field were useful in treating eating disorders. In any case, whether addiction or not, obesity and eating disorders can be serious, and consultation with a physician is needed.

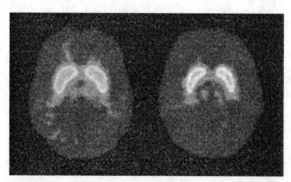

Figure 10-2   D2 dopamine receptors are reduced in obese subjects. PET scans of D2 dopamine receptors showed that the receptors are lower in obese subjects (right side) compared to normal subjects (left side). The relative size and level of the bright area shows the levels of receptors. The larger and brighter the area, the more receptors it has. This is similar to what is found in addicted subjects. A review of Chapter 7 (Figures 7-1 and 7-2) might be helpful. (Reprinted from The Lancet, 357, Gene-Jack Wang, Nora D. Volkow, Jean Logan, Naomi R. Pappas, Christopher T. Wong, Wel Zhu, Noelwah Netusll, and Joanna S. Fowler, Brain dopamine and obesity, 354-357, Copyright [2001], with permission from Elsevier.)

Scares and Excuses

Is referring to someone as an "addict" used as a scare tactic to motivate people who have a problem with obesity (or another behavior)? Calling someone an addict can certainly get his or her attention. But it seems unlikely that this tactic is done by professionals who are certified to treat people with problems. It does seem possible that well-meaning friends or family members might do this. They might even be justified, but it can backfire, creating more fear that only hinders getting treatment.

The reverse question is also important—is the label "addict" used by some as an excuse to continue their self-destructive behavior that is difficult to stop. "I'm an addict" is a declaration that seems to reduce harsh judgments about people doing repetitive, destructive behaviors. This seems to be true particularly if you can say that it's genetic. "My parents were the same way." That seems to be a great excuse. However, placing the blame solely on genetics is not a good excuse, not only because heredity is only one of many risk factors, but also because a genetic predisposition does not guarantee a life of addiction

Summary

There are several extreme behaviors such as pathological gambling, excessive sexual activity, binge eating, and others (excessive Internet use, shopping, and so on) that can be consuming; they take a lot of time, energy, and resources, and can result in significant personal distress and negative consequences for the individual. They might not be accepted as addictions in the strict scientific sense, although it seems that they exhibit many of the important signs found in drug-addicted individuals. Nevertheless, this comparison with drug abuse can be informative and helpful. Treatment methods that are successful for drug users might be useful for them as well, but it is best left to the experts to decide on a course of treatment.

Endnotes

[1]   Actually, that is a simplified definition that is useful, particularly
      for those who are wondering about having a problem with drugs;
      however, the definition used by professionals for purposes of diag-
      nosis is more detailed and contains more elements. For example,
      they question the amount of time that the user has been involved
      in the activity, how many times the user has tried to stop doing the
      drug, whether the user needs to take more drug to get the same
      effect, whether the user has withdrawal, and it asks for a more
      detailed description of the negative consequences. These are
      described in the *DSM-IV TR* and in Endnote 1 in Chapter 1,
      "What's In This Book, and Why Should I Read It?" A useful sum-
      mary of behavioral addictions is in Grant J.E. et al. "Introduction
      to Behavioral Addictions." *Am J Drug Alc Abuse*, 36: 233–241,
      2010. If someone has a concern about addiction, he or she should
      consult a professional.

[2]   Some examples of studies on gambling are as follows: Breiter, H.C
      et al. "Functional Imaging of Neuronal Responses to Expectancy
      and Experience of Monetary Gains and Losses." *Neuron*, 30:
      619–639, 2001; Goudriaan, A.E et al. "Brain Activation Patterns
      Associated with Cue Reactivity and Craving in Abstinent Problem
      Gamblers." *Addiction Biology*, 15: 491–503, 2010; Reuter, J. et al.
      "Pathological Gambling Is Linked to Reduced Activation of the
      Mesolimbic Reward System." *Nature Neurosci*, 8: 147–148, 2005;
      Van Holst, R.J. et al. "Brain Imaging Studies in Pathological
      Gambling." *Curr Psychiatry Rep*, 12: 418–425, 2010.

[3]   Some publications that touch on the issue of sexual addiction are
      as follows: Kelley, A.E. and K.C. Berridge. "The Neuroscience of
      Natural Rewards: Relevance to Addictive Drugs." *J Neurosci*,
      22(9): 3306–3311, 2002; Potenza, M.N. "Should Addictive
      Disorders Include Nonsubstance-Related Conditions?" *Addic-
      tion*, 101 (Suppl 1): 142–151, 2006; Schneider, J.P. and R.R. Irons.
      "Assessment and Treatment of Addictive Sexual Disorders:

Relevance for Chemical Dependency Relapse." *Subst Use Misuse*, 36(13): 1795–820, 2001.

4   Volkow, N.D. and C.P. O'Brien. "Issues for DSM-V: Should Obesity Be Included as a Brain Disorder?" *Amer Journ of Psychiatry*, 164: 708–710, 2007. Avena, N.M. et al. "Sugar and Fat Bingeing Have Notable Differences in Addictive-Like Behavior." *Journal of Nutrition*, 139: 623–628, 2011. Corsica, J.A. and M.L. Pelchat. "Food Addiction: True or False?" *Curr Opin Gastroenterol*, 26: 165–169, 2010. Rogers, P.J. and H.J. Smit. "Food Craving and Food Addiction: A Critical Review of the Evidence from a Biopsychosocial Perspective." *Pharmacol Biochem Behav*, 66: 3–14, 2000.

11

What Else Do Drugs Do to Me?

"I was a heavy drinker for years, ignoring all the warnings about chronic alcoholism. Now, my doctor says that I've got end-stage liver disease with little chance for a cure. I'm kicking myself now. Why did I ever start drinking in the first place?"

Although each drug has its own particular, seductive attraction, each one has some bad side effects. This chapter is mainly about the side effects of the substances rather than the rewarding and reinforcing effects. But the addicting properties of a substance and the harm it causes can be related (see Figure 11-1). Chapter 1, "What's in This Book, and Why Should I Read It?" lists many of the abused drugs and provides a reference to a site where more information can be found about each drug. Remember that the effects of drugs are dose-dependent and time-dependent, meaning that the effects the user experiences depend on how much of the drug the user has had, the amount of time since the last dose, and for how long overall the user has been taking it. There is individual variability in responding to drugs, as they affect some people differently. Many drug users use multiple drugs at the same time; of course, this makes things worse. Read on, and heed the fear in your heart!

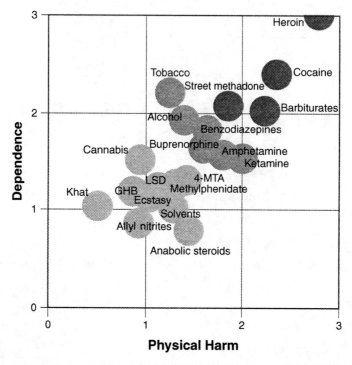

Figure 11-1   The relationship between the addicting properties of a substance and the physical harm that it causes to organs and bodily systems. Efforts have been made to relate addiction (dependence) and physical harm, and, according to one of the devised procedures, there is a relationship. In general, the more addicting a substance, the more harm it can cause, which makes sense. But it is not a perfect relationship. Tobacco more readily produces addiction than it causes harm, whereas anabolic steroids tend to produce more harm relative to their addicting properties. Not all of the drugs in this figure have been discussed in this book. Note that according to this classification scheme, heroin and cocaine are number one and two in both addiction and harm. (Graphical summary from Table 3, Nutt, D et al. "Development of a Rational Scale to Assess the Harm of Drugs of Potential Misuse. *The Lancet*, 369: 1047, 2007, as described in http://en.wikipedia.org/wiki/Cocaine#Acute.)

Alcohol

Alcohol is practically ubiquitous, and this availability creates serious difficulties for the abuser. Alcohol, in certain ways, is one of the most dangerous of the abused drugs. It interferes with judgment and performance, promotes aggressive behavior, is associated with accidents and fatalities, and changes brain structure, function, and chemical makeup (see Figure 11-2). In the emergency room, about 50 percent of patients have alcohol in their blood to varying levels. Forty-four percent of fatal motor vehicle accidents and about 30 percent of fatal falls in the home involve alcohol. It is often found in perpetrators of violent crimes such as murder and brutal domestic disputes. Pregnant mothers who use alcohol put their unborn babies at risk for Fetal Alcohol Syndrome that can cause brain damage and other abnormalities in the infant.

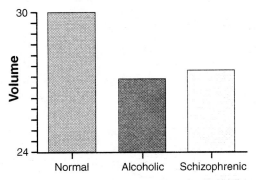

Figure 11-2   The volume of the prefrontal cortex is significantly reduced in alcoholics and is comparable to that in schizophrenics who are serious, chronic, mentally ill patients. The reduction in this brain region is likely associated with a loss of emotional regulation, degradation of judgment, and loss of inhibitions. (Summarized from Mathalon, D.H. et al. Compounded Brain Volume Deficits in Schizophrenia-Alcoholism Comorbidity. *Arch of Gen Psych*, 60: 245–252, 2003.)

Blood levels of alcohol and their association with its behavioral and physiologic effects have been thoroughly studied. Drinking even relatively small amounts of alcohol elevates one's mood, reduces anxiety, and makes you tired. Very large amounts of alcohol can produce respiratory depression that can be followed by coma and even death. Cases of this type have been found where large amounts of alcohol were almost forcibly taken, for example, at a hazing party. Rare complications of alcohol ingestion include an alcohol-induced psychotic disorder with hallucinations and persecutory delusions, and a life-threatening disease called Wernicke's encephalopathy, which is characterized by mental confusion and loss of muscle control. These require immediate treatment.

The best known complication of long-term use of alcohol is liver disease, of which there are two types, fatty liver and liver cirrhosis. These can lead to liver failure and result in expensive medical care or death. Chronic drinking is also associated with vitamin B and thiamin deficiencies. Vitamin B deficiency can manifest as peripheral neuropathies, which is damage to peripheral nerves in the arms and legs. Thiamin deficiency can cause a short-term memory loss syndrome called Korsakoff's syndrome. Again, these serious problems require medical attention.

Heavy drinkers who stop imbibing can experience a severe withdrawal syndrome called delirium tremens (the DTs). After a few hours of abstaining from alcohol, shakiness, sweating, and palpitations appear. One to two days after abstinence, the DTs appear, which include hallucinations, seizures, and sometimes a sensation of insects crawling over the skin. Five to 15 percent of subjects in DTs actually die. Withdrawal from alcohol is obviously very serious, especially in those who drink larger quantities.

Other conditions that can be caused by or made worse by alcohol include: skin conditions, shaking of the limbs, high blood pressure, esophageal reflux, stomach ulcers, gastritis, reduced endocrine function in certain organs, autoimmune diseases, gout, and blood disorders. *Overall, alcohol is certainly one of the most dangerous drugs*, and chronic alcoholism is quite a toxic life style. It is true that light or moderate drinking can be beneficial. It has been associated with lower risks of heart disease, death from a heart attack, some strokes, gallstones, and perhaps even diabetes. But, if someone can't limit drinking and has a tendency to drink more and more, perhaps the risk of harm does not outweigh the potential benefit. A discussion with your doctor can provide helpful guidance.

As has been discussed earlier in this book, drugs of abuse interfere with normal neurotransmission, and alcohol is the same. Alcohol affects several neurotransmitter systems, notably the one for GABA, an inhibitory neurotransmitter. There are several subtypes of GABA receptors, and alcohol enhances the function of the GABA-A receptor. The drug also blocks some of the receptors for glutamate, an excitatory neurotransmitter. The enhancement of inhibition and blockade of excitation underlie the depressant actions of alcohol. Interactions with other neurotransmitters such as acetylcholine and serotonin have been noted as well.

Nicotine

When we talk about nicotine, we are basically talking about smoking, because nicotine is the addictive ingredient in cigarettes that promotes repeated smoking. Experiments have shown that the rate and frequency of smoking are adjusted to keep blood levels of nicotine in a certain range where the rewarding effects are experienced. A first cigarette usually produces negative reactions like choking and stomach upset, but with continued use, these negative feelings subside, and the addicting properties of nicotine begin to take hold. Nicotine stimulates receptors for the neurotransmitter acetylcholine, specifically the nicotinic receptors. Stimulation of these receptors causes a release of dopamine in the nucleus accumbens, a neural effect common with many other addicting drugs.

The behavioral effects of nicotine are subtle and less of a worry compared to other drugs. The drug alleviates anxiety and stress, reduces aggression and anger, and causes a pleasant state of relaxation and euphoria. These effects tend to be positive, but it has become clear that smoking produces a state of dependence. In fact, both animals and humans self-administer it, and tolerance occurs. There is a withdrawal syndrome, and those who try to stop smoking often relapse. Somewhere between a third and a half of smokers become dependent.

Withdrawal signs include craving and depression, and it may be that some smokers try to treat their depression by smoking. Additional signs of withdrawal include weight gain, insomnia, anxiety, irritability, restlessness, and difficulty in concentration. Smoking is so widespread that probably most of us have known friends or family members who experience these withdrawal signs. Smoking tobacco is more of a problem than ingesting pure nicotine. Our lungs take a serious battering from constituents of smoke and carbon monoxide, and other organs are affected as well. Dr. Dorothy Hatsukami and colleagues have noted that the level of exposure to lung toxins, even though real, is variable among individuals,[1] and because one heavy smoker is apparently okay does not mean that others will be okay. The fatal damage done by smoking is described in Table 11-1. Fortunately, laws have been enacted that have raised the price of cigarettes, which makes them less available. Other laws have caused manufacturers to advertise the risk of cancer on each pack. Treatments for nicotine dependence, which are vital for public health, are covered in Chapter 13, "Treatment: How Do I Get Better?"

TABLE 11-1   Causes of Death Attributable to Smoking in Men and Women During the Period 1997–2001

Cause of Death	Men	Women
Cancers	104,219	54,310
Heart disease	84,367	53,612
Lung disease	54,319	47,135
Birth problems	523	387
Secondhand smoke	15,536	22,576

Cancers include oral, esophageal, stomach, pancreatic, tracheal, cervical, urinary, and leukemia. Heart diseases include ischemia, atherosclerosis, aneurysm, and others. Lung diseases include pneumonia, influenza, bronchitis, emphysema, and chronic airway obstruction. Birth problems include short pregnancy, low birth weight, respiratory distress syndrome, and sudden infant death syndrome. Secondhand smoke deaths include those from lung cancer and ischemic heart disease. The total number of deaths exceed 435,000. Aside from these deaths, chronic illnesses cause much misery and expense. (Adapted from "Annual Smoking-Attributable Mortality, Years of Potential Life Lost, and Productivity Losses, United States, 1997–2001," found at http://www.cdc.gov/mmwr/preview/mmwrhtml/mm5425a1.htm, accessed February 7, 2011.)

As mentioned in Chapter 4, "The ABCs of Drug Action in the Brain," nicotine acts at receptors for the neurotransmitter acetylcholine. Historically, acetylcholine was the first neurotransmitter that was discovered, which opened a doorway into the brain that has lead to many major discoveries. Acetylcholine acts at two major types of receptors: the nicotinic receptor and the muscarinic receptor. These subtypes were discovered originally using the substances nicotine and muscarine, which are derived from plants, and how the receptors subtypes got their name. Nicotinic receptors are ion channel receptors, and muscarinic receptors are G-protein coupled receptors (see Chapter 4, Figure 4-2).

Marijuana (Cannabis)

Imagine that several students are preparing for an exam. They take a study break and smoke a joint, saying that it relaxes them and they do better on tests when they aren't uptight. They confidently go back to studying. Could they be wrong?

Marijuana is the most widely used illicit drug. A recent survey by the National Institute on Drug Abuse found that more than 20 percent of high school seniors have used marijuana within the last 30 days! Echoing the previous paragraph is the question of whether it's use affects student performance. Marijuana or the hemp plant (cannabis sativa) is often smoked or eaten to get high. A major active ingredient is delta-9-THC (tetrahydrocannabinol), but there are probably others such as cannabidiol. The strength or percent of the plant that is drug has increased over the past few decades, presumably because of selection. Several different strains of the plant are known. Dronabinol (synthetic THC, whose proprietary name is Marinol) is a marketed medication indicated for appetite stimulation and reduction of vomiting. Hashish, an extract of the plant that is a more pure form of the drug, is made of resinous secretions of the plants which are dried, compressed, and smoked. Delta-9-THC and other ingredients act at receptors for anandamide (and other substances referred to as endogenous cannabinoids), a naturally occurring neurotransmitter in the brain.

The psychological effects at recreational doses of marijuana include euphoria, a sense of well being, and relaxation. But there are also problematic effects such as disorientation, lack of concentration, impaired learning and memory, sedation, panic reactions, and paranoia. The physiological effects are the well known reddening of the eyes, dry mouth and throat, the "munchies" (increased appetite), vasodilation, increased heart rate, urinary retention, constipation, and loss of coordination. Withdrawal symptoms have been reported and include craving, mood changes, headache, weight gain, and sleep disturbances.[2] It is interesting that the quantity of tar inhaled and the amount of carbon monoxide absorbed is three to five times greater than what occurs with tobacco smokers! National surveys from 2005–2007 indicate positive associations between duration of marijuana use and bronchitis and lung cancer, as well as anxiety, depression, and sexually transmitted diseases.[3]

Back to the students described at the beginning of this section. Does smoking pot while you are studying help? No! It doesn't. Effects of the drug include, as mentioned, impairment of concentration, learning, and memory. The students are worse off. Consider a study published on airline pilots who were allowed to smoke marijuana in order to test its effects. They smoked a cigarette containing 20 mg of delta-9-THC, and had their performance examined in a flight simulator. Impairments were found up to 24 hours (a full day) later. The effect of the drug did wear off but it took a long time.[4] So, beware! Impairments can last a long time. If someone has a demanding task or job or a role as a parent, can he or she afford this risk? Someone might argue that the dose the pilots took was higher than one normally takes or that the flight simulator was especially sensitive. Nevertheless, the dangers are real.

"Medical marijuana" is the use of the plant, its extracts, or its ingredients as a physician-recommended medicine. Its documented effects include reduction of nausea and vomiting, stimulation of appetite, and reduction of the symptoms of glaucoma. There are also recent studies of the use of THC in treating various cancers, opioid dependence, and even Alzheimer's disease. The use of marijuana as medicine, or some aspects of it, is controversial in some circles.

Cocaine

Sigmund Freud, the founder of psychoanalysis, was one of the first scientists to experiment with cocaine, which comes from the leaves of the *Erythroxylon coca* plant. He was impressed with the stimulant properties of the drug, and because these properties were opposite to the depressant properties of alcohol and opiates, he reportedly proposed that cocaine be used as an antidote or cure for alcoholism or opiate addiction. He even suggested this to some friends who took his advice. Unfortunately, Freud realized his mistake when cocaine proved to be addicting. This highlights the fact that different addicting drugs can have different acute effects—even opposite ones—and yet, they share the same addicting property. Fortunately, today we have behavioral tests in animals that detect possible addicting substances before they are given to people.

Cocaine can be taken by chewing coca leaves where the drug is absorbed in the mouth, although this is hardly a concern in this country. When the pure form is available as a powder, it can be snorted into the nose, eaten, or dissolved and injected intravenously. The latter is the preferred route among experienced users because it more readily produces a rush of sensations. Crack cocaine, or the free base form of the drug, is smoked because heating readily vaporizes cocaine in this form. Smoking and intravenously injecting drugs are the most effective methods for producing high levels of drug in the brain quickly. Intravenous injections send the drugs effectively to the brain, and smoking results in an efficient transfer of drug from the lung to the blood and then to the brain.

Acute injection of cocaine produces arousal, a sense of well being and confidence, improved performance on tasks of alertness, and an increase in heart rate and blood pressure. Higher doses produce euphoria, which is often the goal of drug abusers. Repeated use can result in agitation, paranoia, psychosis, and addiction. Withdrawal, also referred to as the "crash," includes fatigue, depression, anxiety, and craving for the drug. Other important toxicities include irregular heart rhythms and other cardiac problems, oxygen deprivation because cocaine constricts blood vessels, and seizures. An elevation of blood pressure increases the risk of stroke. Other drugs are often taken together with cocaine. Users sometimes add alcohol to the mix to reduce irritability, which many cocaine users suffer. Similarly, cocaine is used with heroin.

In the brain, at the level of neurotransmission, cocaine blocks the transporters for dopamine, serotonin, and norepinephrine, which increase the amount of neurotransmitter in the synapse and increases the synaptic action of the neurotransmitters (see Chapter 4, Figure 4-4). But the addicting properties of cocaine are attributed to a blockade of only the dopamine transporter.[5] I discovered this along with Dr. Mary Ritz and others when it was shown that the most potent cocaine-like compounds in self-administration studies were also potent in blocking the transporter, and vice versa. This study was the culmination of the work of many including Drs. Roy Wise and Nick Goeders, whose studies pointed at dopamine as the key target for cocaine and other psychostimulants.[6] (see also Chapter 4, Endnote 2).

Methamphetamine

Methamphetamine (also known as crank or ice) has been around for many years and has been used to treat obesity, Attention Deficit Hyperactivity Disorder (ADHD), and sleepiness. Its trade names include Adipex, Desoxyn, and Methedrine. It is also a major drug of abuse and a dangerous one at that. There has been literally a torrent of meth abuse, partly because it is highly addicting and partly because it can be synthesized easily, even in your kitchen. Not only is the drug toxic, but the synthesis of it, or "cooking" as it is called, is dangerous. There are many cases of severe burns and injuries to those making the drug. This substance is most similar to amphetamine but its effects are somewhat different. Meth gets into the brain more easily than amphetamine, causes more dopamine to be released into the synapse than amphetamine, and has been associated with more psychotic symptoms than cocaine. It has also been implicated in the development of Parkinson's disease. Its psychostimulant-like effects are similar to those of the other psychostimulants like cocaine and amphetamine. They include increased alertness and wakefulness, elation, euphoria, and elevation of mood.[7]

An outstanding feature of meth toxicity is its capability to severely impair and perhaps destroy dopamine- and serotonin-containing neurons in the brain. Drs. Jean Lud Cadet, Annette Fleckenstein, Syed Ali, Jerry Meyer, and others have carried out many studies on the way meth produces its toxic effects on neurons. Methamphetamine can also have serious implications related to pregnancy, including a shortened pregnancy and a lower birth weight. There might also be postnatal neurological symptoms in the offspring. In users, it can produce a psychosis characterized by grandiose and paranoid delusions, hallucinations, and disordered thoughts. The duration of these episodes can vary from hours to days. A tendency for the user to have rotten teeth is often associated with meth use. Withdrawal from methamphetamine can be serious. Symptoms include depression, anxiety, fatigue, craving, excessive sleep, loss of pleasure, and loss of concentration. The acute onset of withdrawal is sometimes called the "crash."

A vivid description of what the author believed to be meth toxicity is described by Nick Reddy in *Methland* (reprinted by permission of International Creative Management, Inc. Copyright © 2009 by Nick Reding).

"Jarvis is just one of many local legends...staying high on crank for twenty-eight days....By the time I met him, he'd had four heart attacks...couldn't sleep and rarely had an appetite. Almost all his teeth were gone, and those that remained were black and decaying. He was in almost constant pain; his muscles ached and his joints were stiff....One of (his children)...born at the peak of his parents' intravenous meth use, was wearing a colostomy bag by the age of ten.

Unable to shoot up with the finger nubs left him by the lab explosion, Jarvis had taught himself to hold a pipe and lighter so that he could resume his meth habit..."

As already noted, meth produces its addicting effects by targeting the dopamine transporter. However, unlike cocaine, which blocks only the uptake of dopamine but does not promote its release, meth both blocks uptake and promotes the release of the neurotransmitter. Methamphetamine also blocks the transporters for serotonin and norepinephrine, which produces other effects. For example, blockade of the norepinephrine transporter increases the availability of norepinephrine and therefore increases blood pressure.

A separate section is not devoted to amphetamine because it is similar to both cocaine and methamphetamine. It affects nerve cells the way meth does.

Xanax, Valium, and Other Sedatives

An important class of drugs that are among the most widely prescribed in the world is the benzodiazepines. This is a general chemical name for drugs that share certain chemical structures and properties. Trade names of drugs in this class include Xanax, Klonopin, Valium, and Ativan. They are used as sedatives and as sleep inducers or hypnotics. As sedatives, they reduce anxiety and have a calming effect; as sleep inducers, they cause drowsiness that facilitates the onset of sleep. Each drug can be used as a sedative and as a sleep inducer, the only difference being the dose that is used. Sleep induction requires a higher dose than is required for calming. These drugs are relatively safe in overdose situations and have replaced older drugs such as the barbiturates. Sometimes these drugs are used before various diagnostic or surgical procedures to produce both calming and amnesia.

Important side effects are those expected of a sedating agent. They can cause increased reaction times, impairment of mental and motor functions, amnesia, and accidents. When taken during the day for anxiety, the dose is important because the drugs can produce excessive sleepiness. Some drug users take these drugs to get high, and others take them to treat anxiety and irritability associated with use of other drugs. Chronic use, say over several months, can lead to addiction. Withdrawal symptoms include anxiety, agitation, sleep disturbance, muscle cramps, and dizziness. However, if the addict has been using high doses, seizures and delirium are also possible.

This class of drugs acts at the GABA-A receptors just like alcohol. By themselves, they do not stimulate the receptors, but they enhance the action of the naturally occurring neurotransmitter GABA. Patients who abuse alcohol are also more likely to abuse benzodiazepines.

Oxycontin and Other Opiates

Oxycontin is a popular drug of abuse that falls in the opiate class that also contains heroin and morphine. Opiate drugs are used legitimately in the treatment of pain and are mainstays in that area. But, the same neuronal systems that alter pain also produce feelings of euphoria and well being, which lead to abuse and addiction. Tolerance occurs, and there is a significant withdrawal syndrome when the drugs are not taken. Opiates produce some unpleasant effects including nausea, vomiting, and sedation, particularly in people not addicted or not being treated for pain.

Because of the medical importance of this group of compounds, there are many different opiates produced and made available for treating humans. Heroin is one of the most dangerous opiates. It is quickly converted to its active metabolite and gets into the brain rapidly. There is a period of intense euphoria followed by feelings of tranquility. Withdrawal produces a craving for the drug, anxiety, insomnia, irritability, cramps and muscle aches. Withdrawal can last five to ten days and is unpleasant, although it is usually not life threatening. Overdose is a danger and if death occurs, it is often due to respiratory depression. The mortality rate for heroin addicts on the street is very high, as it is for users of other drugs as well. Opiates are often used in combination with other drugs. For example, it is often taken after or with cocaine (called a speedball) to quell the agitation and irritability produced by cocaine.

Drug users who inject opiates (and other drugs for that matter) can obtain serious infections associated with using contaminated and dirty needles. These include ugly skin abscesses, hepatitis, tuberculosis, and AIDS. They are also at higher risk for sexually transmitted diseases. Opiate drugs work by stimulating receptors for the opioid peptide neurotransmitters such as enkephalin and endorphin, which are chemicals that occur naturally in the brain.

Ecstasy and "Club" Drugs

Ecstasy, sometimes called X, is an interesting substance that has both stimulant effects like cocaine and amphetamine, but also has hallucinogenic or psychedelic effects like LSD. It is mainly popular among younger drug users, often at dances called raves. Ecstasy used to be considered useful in psychotherapy to promote compassion and insights, but hard data on this is lacking. Its laboratory name is methylenedioxymethamphetamine (MDMA).

Its effects are reported to include empathy, insight, and feelings of closeness to others. But it also produces, as psychological tests have shown, increased depression and anxiety, impulsiveness, and hostility. Its toxicity is serious in that it seems to deplete or destroy axons and nerve terminals that contain serotonin, perhaps forever, in animal studies. Drs. Perry Renshaw, Scott Lukas, and others have found a reduction in the size of the cerebral cortex in human MDMA abusers.[8] Paradoxically, some findings suggest that the behavior of human users does not seem to be a problem, but there is a concern about the future in that brain changes might presage significant, future problems. Although MDMA has not emerged as a significant addiction problem so far, there is concern that it might. It can result in increased heart rate and blood pressure, and there have been reported overdoses that have resulted in death. MDMA has diverse effects in the brain. It can block serotonin transporters, resulting in changes in neurotransmission, and it can bind to a variety of neuro-transmitter receptors. MDMA is basically an analogue of ampheta-mine and methamphetamine, and there are other analogues of amphetamine that are abused. For example, MDA has similar prop-erties to MDMA.

Ecstasy is known as a club drug along with others substances that include GHB, Rohypnol, and ketamine. GHB and Rohypnol (roofies) are sedating, and Rohypnol can produce unconsciousness and amne-sia. Ketamine distorts perceptions and feelings. They are called club drugs because they are sometimes used heavily at dance clubs, bars, parties, and other gatherings.

PCP (Phencyclidine)

PCP (also known as angel dust or rocket fuel) is a synthetic substance that was originally made to be used as an anesthetic. But, it had nega-tive psychological effects and was never approved for human use. It is called a dissociative drug because it produces feelings of detachment and disconnection from the environment. It also causes distortions of sights and sounds, and disordered thinking reminiscent of schizo-phrenia. For this reason, animals given PCP have been considered a model of that disease. At higher doses, it produces agitation, poten-tially life threatening seizures, and respiratory depression. There are press reports describing wildly aggressive behavior and bizarre acts of violence by those using the drug. For example, one anecdotal report describes a man on PCP who broke both of his wrists trying to get out of handcuffs. Another strange story involves a man on PCP who cut off parts of his face, including his nose, lips, and ears, and fed them to his dogs![9] Although these behaviors might depend on a violence-prone personality or preexisting mental illness of the drug user just as much as on the drug itself, PCP can be a dangerous substance.

Microscopic signs of nerve toxicity are found in users that can lead to persistent brain damage. PCP works by blocking the NMDA subtype of the receptors for the neurotransmitter glutamate.

Caffeine

We don't think of caffeine as a drug, but it does produce intoxication and withdrawal signs, and it is perhaps the most widely used psychoactive (mind-altering) substance in the world. It is a stimulant, but it is different from the psychostimulants like cocaine because its mechanism of action is different. It does not affect the dopamine system directly. Rather, caffeine blocks subtypes of receptors for another neurotransmitter, adenosine.

Caffeine is called a mild stimulant and is found in coffee, tea, sodas, chocolate, and some medicines. It increases alertness and wakefulness, and it produces feelings of increased energy. It improves reactions and reaction time and enhances cognitive functioning. Within reasonable limits, it is considered safe, and you wouldn't mind if your pilot was taking it! However, if a high dose—perhaps more than three cups—is taken, unpleasant symptoms appear that include restlessness, nervousness, anxiety, insomnia, high blood pressure, frequent urination, and stomach complaints. Yet higher doses can produce muscle twitching, rapid heartbeat, abnormal heart rhythms, and a rambling thought pattern. There is some concern that the current trend among energy drinks to increase caffeine to higher levels may be somewhat dangerous.

Tolerance does occur, and, after drinking it for some time, you might need a higher dose to get the same expected effect. After becoming accustomed to as few as one or two cups per day, cessation of caffeine intake can produce withdrawal that consists mainly of feelings of fatigue and tiredness. Withdrawal can also include, particularly after higher doses, headache, nausea, and vomiting, but the latter is rare. Because few caffeine drinkers report loss of control of intake or have a great difficulty in stopping caffeine use, it is not listed as an addicting stimulant.[10]

Summary

The seven classes of abused and addicting drugs discussed in this chapter also have many additional and varying effects on the body and brain. Although addiction is a serious effect of using drugs, there are other effects of the drugs that are also serious. Because each drug class is different and because each drug in the class can be somewhat different from the others in its class, there are many different kinds of side effects. Some are subtle, such as the reduction in cognitive ability after marijuana, and some are seriously toxic, such as the increase in risk for respiratory disease and cancer after smoking. Although therapeutic medications prescribed by doctors for various illnesses also have side effects, the patient can stop taking them when trouble appears, but the addicts do not stop. They tolerate the side effects and the problems can get serious and chronic. Therefore, it is of extreme importance for everyone to recognize not only the threat of addiction, but also the other harmful and potentially life-threatening properties of these drugs.

Endnotes

[1]   For example, see Hecht S.S. et al. "Similar Uptake of Lung Carcinogens by Smokers of Regular, Light, and Ultralight Cigarettes." *Cancer Epidemio Biomarkers Prev*, 14: 693–698, 2005.

[2]   An example of a study showing withdrawal symptoms from cannabis is: Levin K.H. et al. Cannabis Withdrawal Symptoms in Nontreatment-Seeking Adult Cannabis Smokers." *Drug Alc Dep* 111: 120–127. This is an interesting topic because cannabis withdrawal is noted in the *DSM-IV-TR*, because of uncertainties about its clinical importance.

3   Han B. et al. "Associations between Duration of Illicit Drug Use
    and Health Conditions: Results from the 2005–2007 National
    Surveys on Drug Use and Health." *Ann Epidemiol*, 20: 289–97.
    The National Institute on Drug Abuse has recently produced a
    report, "Marijuana Abuse," which can be viewed at www.nida.
    nih.gov/ResearchReports/Marijuana/default.html, accessed on
    June 1, 2011.

4   It has been found that marijuana smoking impaired pilot perform-
    ance for up to 24 hours. Nine active pilots smoked one cigarette
    containing 20 mg of delta-9-THC, and a placebo (no drug) ciga-
    rette. Using an aircraft simulator, seven of the nine pilots showed
    impairment at 24 hours after smoking the drug. There was no
    impairment at 48 hours after or before smoking the drug.
    Interestingly, only one of the seven said he felt the drug. Thus, sig-
    nificant impairment can be maintained for up to 24 hours after
    smoking marijuana, even though you might not be aware of any
    effect of the drug at that time. It can be argued that most users do
    not take that much drug or that the simulator test was especially
    sensitive. In any case, the negative cognitive effects of marijuana
    can last many hours. From Leirer, V.O. et al. "Marijuana Carry-
    Over Effects on Aircraft Pilot Performance." *Aviat Space Enviro
    Med*, 62: 221–227, 1991.

5   Cocaine is addicting because it blocks the dopamine transporter.
    This was discovered in an experiment that compared the potency
    of the addicting properties of several cocaine-like drugs and in
    their capabilities to block transporters. The potency of the drugs
    in causing addiction in an animal model correlated only with their
    capabilities to block the dopamine transporter, not other trans-
    porters. Only cocaine-like compounds and methylphenidate that
    do not cause release of dopamine, but only block uptake of
    dopamine, were included in the study. See Ritz, M.C. et al.
    "Cocaine Receptors on Dopamine Transporters Are Related to
    Self-Administration of Cocaine." *Science* 237: 1219–1223, 1987.

[6] The following is a brief summary of the history of the dopamine story and drug addiction. It is a personal communication from Dr. Roy Wise, a longtime, productive researcher in this field.

The earliest work was by Olds (a) who showed that nonselective drugs like chlorpromazine and reserpine (whose effects included a blunting of dopamine's effects) antagonized electrical brain stimulation reward. Larry Stein generated a theory of reward that proposed that norepinephrine was the key neurotransmitter, but this was not supported by subsequent data (b, c). When selective dopamine antagonists became available, they, and selective destruction of dopamine-containing neurons showed effects on reward. This implicated dopamine and not norepinephrine or other neurotransmitters in brain stimulation reward (d, e). Roy Pickens and Harris were the first to suggest that the substrates of brain stimulation reward and psychostimulant reward were perhaps the same (f).

Bob Yokel and I (g) and Davis and Smith (h) were the first to show that amphetamine lost its rewarding action if the dopamine system was selectively blocked, and Harriet de Wit and I (i) and Risner and Jones (j) showed the same result with cocaine. Dave Roberts showed that selective dopamine (but not norepinephrine) lesions disrupted cocaine reward (k). These were the first studies to show that dopamine function was necessary for cocaine and amphetamine reward. Bob Yokel and I then showed that a dopamine agonist, apomorphine, (a compound that directly stimulated dopamine receptors) was self-administered (g, l), which confirmed that dopamine activation was also sufficient for drug-related reward. Ritz et al. (m) took the story further by showing that the initial site of action of cocaine and the psychostimulants—specifically for their rewarding and reinforcing actions—was the dopamine transporter rather than some other site. Initial work in knockout mice suggested that cocaine might still be rewarding in animals lacking the dopamine transporter (n), but more recent work questions this finding and shows, rather, the opposite (o).

(a) J. Olds, K. F. Killam, P. Bach y Rita, *Science* 124, 265 (1956). (b) L. Stein, *J Psychiat Res* 8, 345 (1971). (c) S. K. Roll, *Science* 168, 1370 (1970). (d) A. S. Lippa, S. M. Antelman, A. E. Fisher, D. R. Canfield, *Pharmacology Biochemistry and Behavior* 1, 23 (1973). (e) G. Fouriezos, R. A. Wise, Brain Research 103, 377 (Feb 20, 1976). (f) R. Pickens, W. C. Harris, *Psychopharmacologia* 12, 158 (1968). (g) R. A. Yokel, R. A. Wise, *Science* 187, 547 (Feb 14, 1975). (h) W. M. Davis, S. G. Smith, *Journal of Pharmacy and Pharmacology* 27, 540 (1975). (i) H. de Wit, R. A. Wise, *Can J Psychol* 31, 195 (1977). (j) M. E. Risner, B. E. Jones, *Psychopharmacology* 71, 83 (1980). (k) D. C. S. Roberts, M. E. Corcoran, H. C. Fibiger, *Pharmacology Biochemistry and Behavior* 6, 615 (1977). (l) R. A. Yokel, R. A. Wise, *Psychopharmacology (Berl)* 58, 289 (July 19, 1978). (m) Ritz M.C. et al., 1987. *Science* 237: 1219–1223. (n) B. A. Rocha et al., *Nature Neuroscience* 1, 132 (1998). (o) M. Thomsen, D. D. Han, H. H. Gu, S. B. Caine, *J Pharmacol Exp Ther* 331, 204 (2009).

[7] The *Oregonian* newspaper did a special report on methamphetamine, which is found at the site http://www.pbs.org/wgbh/pages/frontline/meth/body/. Deputy Brett King, from Oregon's Multnomah County Sheriff's Dept, used mug shots to compare the faces of meth users before and after they used the drug. The changes in the eyes, overall expression, teeth, and body weight were astonishing. Methamphetamine, like the other most addicting drugs, can take over your life to the point when you fail to maintain your health. See also http://www.oregonlive.com/news/oregonian/photos/gallery.ssf?cgi-bin/view_gallery.cgi/olive/view_gallery.ata?g_id=2927, accessed on July 1, 2011.

8   For example, Cowan R.L. et al. "Reduced Cortical Gray Matter Density in Human MDMA (Ecstasy) Users." *Drug Alcohol Depend,*= 72: 225–235, 2003.

9   See http://www.snopes.com/horrors/drugs/facepeel.asp for a discussion of this amazing story.

10 *DSM-IV-TR*, Fourth edition, Washington DC: American Psychiatric Association, 2000.

12

Women and Adolescents

A desperate young woman who has been addicted to crack cocaine for some years is considering entering treatment—for a second time. The last time, it just didn't work. "Maybe I just wasn't ready," she said. "I have a very irrational fear of gaining back a lot of the weight that I lost when I started using crack. Extra weight has been a lifelong problem for me and I have a hard time dealing with it." Also, there were many more men than women in her treatment group. "Whether they did or not, the men didn't seem to have much sympathy for my problems." She also felt her responses to issues and questions were a little different from the men's, and she withdrew emotionally. "I never had much confidence around older men, and for personal reasons, I'm a little afraid of them." But, this time, with the advice of friends, she has decided to ask for a treatment group or program that focuses on women. "Maybe this is petty, but I really need all the help I can get right now."

A recent, popular book tells us that men and women are from different planets! Well, we certainly are different in many, obvious ways, and sometimes in ways that are not so obvious. Even our brain sizes are slightly different from an early age. No data has informed us whether the small difference in brain size confers any special attribute on either sex, and there is no reason to assume that it does. After all, there is evidence that the size of the Neanderthal adult brain was larger than ours.[1] But this difference in brain size emphasizes how pervasive these sex differences, even though small, can be.

Many studies over many years have shown that there are important differences between how men and women react to drugs. Female alcoholics begin drinking later in life than men. Because they appear for treatment at about the same age, it is suggested that alcoholism progresses faster in women. Women alcoholics drink less than men at about 9 drinks per week compared to more than 16 drinks for men. They are more likely than men to report a past stressful event as a reason for drinking, and are more likely to have a second diagnosis, particularly depression. They also have a greater history of suicide attempts than either males or nonalcoholic women (about four times more frequent than nonalcoholic women).

The findings with illicit drugs are generally similar, but there are some differences. Drug dependent women enter treatment at a younger age than men. They are more likely to go voluntarily to treatment than men and are more likely to report suicide attempts. Women are more likely to say that stress and anxiety were the cause of relapse, whereas men more often seek the pleasurable effects of the drugs in relapse. Regarding adolescent women using cocaine, the National Household Survey by the National Institute on Drug Abuse found a higher rate of cocaine dependence than in men, and more symptoms with lower doses of the drug. The latter suggests that women are more sensitive than men to cocaine. Among marijuana and opiate users, women again progress to addiction faster than men. Among smokers, women have higher rates of addiction and are more sensitive to nicotine in that they show symptoms at lower doses than men. Women in treatment more often report a concern with weight gain and express a desire for all-women treatment groups.

Women also experience drugs somewhat differently than men. Women report more nervousness than men after intranasal cocaine, experience less euphoria, take more time to feel the effects of a dose of cocaine, and seem to crave more strongly than men in response to cocaine-related cues. There are also reports that they use more of the drug than men.

Because women show different behavioral patterns and responses to some drugs compared to men, there may be sex differences in the parts of the brain that cause drug addiction. Inevitably, this has raised the question of whether treatments need to be tailored specifically to women's needs to be most effective.[2]

Supportive Laboratory Findings

Because of the importance of this topic, there have been many interesting laboratory studies that support the idea of sex differences. For example, female rats show greater behavioral responses than males after cocaine administration. They require lower doses than males to produce the same kind of responses, and the responses last longer than those in males. In cocaine self-administration studies, female rats take cocaine faster and more often than males. There are also sex differences in responses to opiates. Dr. Ann Z. Murphy, her colleagues, and others have noted that morphine is more effective in men than women for treating pain. Interestingly, there are corresponding sex differences in the anatomy of pain pathways in the lower brain and spinal cord.

There doesn't seem to be any doubt that females are different from males when it comes to drug taking. The question is "Why?" The thing that comes to mind most readily is that females have different hormones than men. Estrogen is known as the female hormone, and testosterone is the male hormone. Are the sex differences in drug use based on the hormonal differences? It is now clear that estrogen is a key factor in the sensitivity of females to cocaine and other drugs. This has been shown in basic experiments with animals that manipulate hormone levels in females and males. An effective way of removing or lowering estrogen in females is to surgically remove the ovaries; likewise, the way to remove or lower testosterone in males is to remove the testicles. If there is an effect of removing the ovaries, then the way to see if it is due to estrogen is to give estrogen back to the animals. Table 12-1 shows data from one of the many experiments on this topic. It shows the amount of cocaine taken by animals with and without estrogen and testosterone.

TABLE 12-1 The Female Hormone Estrogen Influences the Intake of Cocaine

Animal Type	Cocaine Intake
OVX + E	14.4 **
OVX	11.0 *
CAST	8.0
SHAM (males)	7.5

By using surgically manipulated males and females, it is possible to test for the influence of sex hormones on various processes. Removing the ovaries (OVX) removes circulating estrogen in females, and removing the testicles (CAST) removes circulating testosterone in males. In cases where OVX changes the animal's behavior, we can test if the change is due to estrogen (E) by adding it back to the animal (OVX + E). Another good comparison is a SHAM male animal where the rats have been subjected to some surgery but nothing has been removed. The data shows that CAST and SHAM males are not statistically different, indicating that testosterone has no influence on cocaine intake. The OVX animals took more cocaine than males, which shows a known sex difference. But there is an effect of E; cocaine intake (0.4 mg/kg) is increased further when E is given (OVX + E). Statistical differences are shown by asterisks. One asterisk indicates OVX females took more cocaine than CAST or SHAM males, and two asterisks indicate that OVX + E females took more cocaine than all of the other groups. (Summarized from Hu, H., H.S. Crombag, T.E. Robinson and J.B. Becker. "Biological Basis of Sex Differences in the Propensity to Self-Administer Cocaine." *Neuropsychopharmacology* 29:81-85, 2004. Data summarized from Figure 12-2.)

SHAM males, males who have had surgery but did not have any organs removed, took about the same amount of cocaine as castrated (CAST) males (see Table 12-1). So, testosterone does not seem to be a factor in drug taking. But there is a marked effect of manipulating estrogen (E) levels. Females who had their ovaries removed (OVX) took more cocaine than males, repeating the known result that females take more cocaine than males under many conditions. Females took even more when estrogen was given as a supplement (OVX + E). This clearly shows that estrogen influences cocaine intake, and this type of experiment has been performed many times in many laboratories with a similar result. Thus, a hormonal mechanism affects the cocaine intake in women, at least to some degree.

Because cocaine and estrogen can have many effects in many different places in the brain, the new questions are: *where* and *how* is estrogen working? Based on the knowledge that cocaine's effects are due to increased dopamine levels in the brain synapses, an initial question is, "Does estrogen work through dopamine?" It turns out that OVX lowers dopamine release, but CAST has no effect. From this, it appears that estrogen can affect dopamine release in brain. Now the question is, *how* does estrogen affect dopamine? Is it a direct effect of estrogen at estrogen receptors on dopamine-containing neurons? Or is it an indirect effect? Answers to these questions are being developed. It has also been noted by Dr. Jill Becker and colleagues that dopamine cannot be the full story behind sex differences and cocaine, and there must be additional factors that contribute to the differences in the brain as well.[3] Someday, with additional research, we will have a better idea of why female brains differ from male brains in their vulnerability to drugs.

Should Treatment Also Be Different?

In a comparison of men and women in a methadone maintenance program, women sometimes relapsed more than men; perhaps there should be more focus and study of relapse factors in women. There also appeared to be sex differences in the responses to buprenorphine or methadone, medications to treat heroin dependence. The exact nature of these differences could influence the way the medications are used when treating women. In a treatment program for smokers (a nicotine replacement program), more women than men thought that the nicotine inhaler was effective. Recall that morphine is more effective in treating pain in men than in women.

Overall, it seems likely that sex has an influence on the response to treatment,[4] and this suggests that there should be an emphasis on understanding the importance of sex differences in treatment. Further studies and improvements in treatment will benefit both

men and women in that treatment will be sex-specific and more efficacious. In any case, if you are a woman and your treatment does not
seem to be going as well as perhaps it is for some men, don't give up.
Keep trying and searching for solutions.

Adolescents

Adolescents do not have mature brains (see Figure 12-1) because
they continue to develop throughout adolescence. This development
continues particularly in the frontal regions that are so critical for
judgment and making appropriate decisions.[5] Not only are frontal
brain regions poorly developed in adolescents, continued drug use
disrupts normal frontal cortex function, and both of these significantly contributes to being an addict. In the chapter on vulnerability,
it was stated that the earlier in life that drug use begins, the greater
the chance of becoming an addict in later life (see Chapter 8, "Could
I Become An Addict?," Figure 8-3). Some children and adolescents
appear to be at greater risk for drug abuse because of various factors
that include genetics, family history of drug use, personality factors,
birth defects, and co-existing emotional problems such as conduct
disorder. Adolescents abuse a number of drugs, and marijuana is the
most often used illicit drug in this age group. Inhalants, a toxic group
of substances, are also often used by adolescents and children.
Alcohol abuse by adolescents is considered a major problem. It is
associated with premature adolescent death, crime, unplanned preg-
nancies, and sexually transmitted diseases. Just as the use of therapeutic medications (for example, antidepressants) in children and
adolescents is of great concern, because of possible long lasting side
effects, drug use with its uncertainties and toxicities is also a significant worry for parents. Thus, the period of adolescence has received
much attention from drug abuse researchers, and appropriately so.
Damage done in adolescence can result in a lifelong disadvantage.

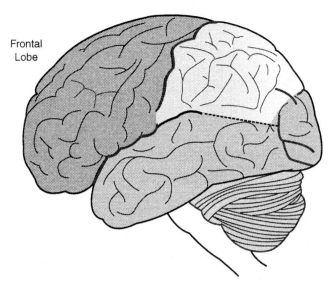

Frontal
Lobe

Figure 12-1   The adolescent frontal lobe is not mature compared to the adult
frontal lobe. The frontal lobe (shaded) makes up the front part of the brain, and
many studies have shown that adolescent frontal lobes (ages 12–16 years)
are not fully developed compared to adult frontal lobes (23–30 years).
Because the frontal cortex serves judgment and executive functions, these
functions develop more slowly in teens than most other functions. In a study
done in monkeys, the innervation of the frontal cortex with dopaminergic neurons continued through adolescence and into early adulthood.[6] (From
http://www.drzukiwski.com/brain-function, accessed on June 15, 2011.)

We know that puberty (adolescence) is a time of great vulnerability to drug abuse in humans. This is likely due to many factors including the immature brain and peer pressure. An interesting finding is
that the adolescent brain seems more sensitive to rewards, and a
teenager is likely to want more of a rewarding substance. This has
been studied in rats that have, for example, access to sweetened condensed milk, a highly rewarding substance to animals. The experiments included breakpoints, which, as discussed earlier are a
measure of reward. Overall, the data in this particular study (see
Figure 12-2) showed that pubertal rats took much more of the milk
than adults. Was milk more desirable in adolescence compared to
adulthood? Probably so. It is something in the brain itself that causes
the difference, but we do not yet fully understand it. It is relevant that
foods are natural rewards and are thought to use many of the same

neuronal circuits in the brain as drugs. Because of this, food data is often interesting to drug researchers.

The data in Figure 8-4 from Chapter 8 comes to mind. Young dopamine neurons respond more than adult neurons to the same stimulus, and it has been shown in many ways that adolescents are different from adults in response to rewards. Having demonstrated higher intake in younger animals suggests that further experimentation will reveal the underlying causes of this enhanced intake. Moreover, having an animal model of this adolescent vulnerability might allow us to test for medications that might be especially efficacious in teen agers. The combination approach of first observing human problems and then modeling and testing the problems in animals is powerful.

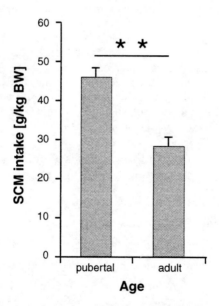

Figure 12-2 Adolescents seek more rewards than adults. This study in rats examined the intake of sweetened condensed milk (SCM) during both puberty and adulthood. The pubertal rat (ages postnatal days 40-60) had a marked increase in milk intake compared to the adult rat (age postnatal day 90). This may help explain why human adolescents are more vulnerable to drug use than those of other ages. The asterisks over the bar indicate that the differences between pubertal and adult are significant. SCM is a substance found to be highly rewarding in animals. (Adapted from Friemel, C.M. et al. "Reward Sensitivity for a Palatable Food Reward Peaks During Pubertal Development in Rats." *Frontiers in Behavioral Neuroscience*, 4: 1-10, Figure 1c, 2010.)

The Elderly

The preceding discussion shows that certain groups of patients, women, and adolescents present special problems for the drug abuse treatment system. The elderly also have some unique issues. The abuse of alcohol and drugs by older adults has been called the invisible epidemic because we know much less about drug use in this population. There are also additional factors that make drug use in the elderly noteworthy. For one, metabolism of alcohol (and other drugs) is slower, meaning that lower doses have stronger effects compared to effects in younger adults. The total amount of water in the body is lower in older adults, and because alcohol occupies this space, its brain concentration is higher in the elderly, resulting in greater effects on the brain with fewer drinks. Older adults often have more chronic health problems that can be made worse by chronic alcohol use. For example, the loss of mental sharpness that occurs with age can be made worse by intoxication, which occurs at lower alcohol doses in the elderly. Also, depression found in the elderly can be made worse by alcohol.

Summary

Various drug effects and toxicities can be significantly different in different age groups and in men compared to women. This is useful information to have, not only for the patients but also for the people treating them. Adolescents, because of greater vulnerability and a full life ahead of them, are an especially important target for prevention efforts. The elderly are often more sensitive to alcohol's effects. There are different elements in various treatment programs that can better address different groups of patients.

Endnotes

[1]   Braun, David. "Neanderthal Brain Size at Birth Sheds Light on Human Evolution. *National Geographic*, September 9, 2008. http://newswatch.nationalgeographic.com/2008/09/09/neanderthal/.

[2]   There is extensive literature on sex diffrences in drug abuse: Becker, J.B. and M. Hu. "Sex Differences in Drug Abuse." *Front Neuroendocrinol*, 29(1): 36–47, 2008; Quinones-Jenab, V. "Why Are Women from Venus and Men from Mars When They Abuse Cocaine?" *Brain Res*, 1126(1): 200–203, 2006; Kosten, T.R., et al. Gender Differences in Response to Intranasal Cocaine Administration to Humans." *Biol Psychiatry*, 39(2): 147–148, 1996; Walker, Q.D., et al. "Sex Differences in Cocaine-Stimulated Motor Behavior: Disparate Effects of Gonadectomy." *Neuropsychopharmacology*, 25(1): 118–130, 2001; White, T.L., A.J. Justice, and H. de Wit. "Differential Subjective Effects of D-amphetamine by Gender, Hormone Levels, and Menstrual Cycle Phase." *Pharmacol Biochem Behav*, 73(4): 729–741, 2002; Ignjatova, L. and M. Raleva. "Gender Difference in the Treatment Outcome of Patients Served in the Mixed-Gender Program." *Bratisl Lek List*, 110(5): 285–289, 2009; Narayanan, S., J.O. Ebbert, and A. Sood. "Gender Differences in Self-Reported Use, Perceived Efficacy, and Interest in Future Use of Nicotine-Dependence Treatments: A Cross-Sectional Survey in Adults at a Tertiary Care Center for Nicotine Dependence." *Gend Med*, 6(2): 362–368, 2009; Ambrose-Lanci, L.M., R.C. Sterling, and E.J. Van Bockstaele. "Cocaine Withdrawal-Induced Anxiety in Females: Impact of Circulating Estrogen and Potential Use of Delta-Opioid Receptor Agonists for Treatment." *J Neurosci Res*, 88(4): 816–824, 2010; Jones, H.E., H. Fitzgerald, and R.E. Johnson. "Males and Females Differ in Response to Opioid Agonist Medications." *Am J Addict*, 14(3): 223–233, 2005; Zhou, W., K.A. Cunningham, and M.L. Thomas. "Estrogen Regulation of Gene Expression in the

Brain: A Possible Mechanism Altering the Response to Psychostimulants in Female Rats. *Brain Res Mol Brain Res*, 100(1-2): 75–83, 2002; Sell, S.L., et al. "Influence of Ovarian Hormones and Estrous Cycle on the Behavioral Response to Cocaine in Female Rats." *J Pharmacol Exp Ther*, 293(3): 879–886, 2000; Walker, Q.D., R. Ray, and C.M. Kuhn. "Sex Differences in Neurochemical Effects of Dopaminergic Drugs in Rat Striatum." *Neuropsychopharmacology*, 31(6): 1193–1202, 2006; Parylak, S.L., et al. "Gonadal Steroids Mediate the Opposite Changes in Cocaine-Induced Locomotion Across Adolescence in Male and Female Rats." *Pharmacol Biochem Behav*, 89(3): 314–323, 2008; Kippin, T.E., et al. "Potentiation of Cocaine-Primed Reinstatement of Drug Seeking in Female Rats During Estrus." *Psychopharmacology (Berl)*, 182(2): 245–252, 2005; Fuchs, R.A., et al. "Influence of Sex and Estrous Cyclicity on Conditioned Cue-Induced Reinstatement of Cocaine-Seeking Behavior in Rats." *Psychopharmacology (Berl)*, 179(3): 662–672, 2005.

[3] Ibid.

[4] Ibid.

[5] For example, see Rosenberg D.R. and Lewis D.A. "Postnatal Maturation of the Dopaminergic Innervation of the Monkey Prefrontal and Motor Cortices." *J Comp Neurol*, 358: 383–400, 1995. See also Sowell E.R. et al. "In Vivo Evidence for Post-Adolescent Brain Maturation in Frontal Regions." *Nature Neuroscience*, 2: 859–861, 1999.

[6] Ibid.

13

Treatment: How Do I Get Better?

Suppose you have been doing drugs for several years, and your life has begun falling apart. Your boss is suspicious over your behavior and absences. Your spouse is fed up and threatening to leave. You owe plenty of money to the banks and your friends. Out of desperation, you talk to your family physician, who has been telling you for months that "It doesn't have to be this way. Get into treatment! Get into treatment!"

Many people are in trouble because they are using drugs, but it *really* doesn't have to be this way. Treatment is available. Some people are confused about what treatment means. It does *not* mean that they will be handcuffed, arrested, locked up, given a prison record, forcibly withdrawn from drugs, and then tossed back into the street! It is going to be much less traumatic and more helpful than they might think. The effectiveness of treatment is well documented. Many people's lives have been saved by timely treatment. Does it always work for every person? Well, some people require several episodes of treatments and relapses before their addiction is successfully treated. Some might drop out of treatment or never get adequate treatment. We might not yet know how to reach these latter subjects, but treatment research goes on and advances are made all the time. There are some factors that predict better success in treatment, such as a lower level of dependence or drug use, a good support system, and a job/career. That is not to say that all of these are absolutely needed, but just that they seem to help. People with none of these characteristics have successfully recovered.

Why Treat? It's Too Expensive

There are significant costs of drug use and addiction. Chapter 1, "What's in This Book, and Why Should I Read It?" (see Figure 1-2) shows how the costs of drug use are distributed. If an individual is contemplating treatment, he or she might feel it is too expensive. But on the other hand, the person probably can't afford not to go into treatment. Also, in many cities treatment can be free, at low cost, or on a sliding scale, so cost is not a valid excuse. Even if it was expensive, it is cheaper to treat than not to treat! That might be surprising but this is what has been found by several studies on different drugs such as alcohol and cocaine. We have a good idea what the costs are to drug users, their families, friends, and society. Assuming reasonable costs for treatment and reasonable recovery rates for drug users, it is clear that treatment is cheaper than allowing drug users to continue on as they are. Some studies say that the savings over a three-year period are multiples of what it costs to treat the individuals compared to leaving them untreated. Treatment is more of an investment than a cost.

What Is Successful Treatment?

When we say that treatment has been successful, does it mean that the patient never takes the drug again? Is it total and permanent abstinence? Well, that is certainly the ideal and would be best. The goal of many treatment groups such as Alcoholics Anonymous (AA) is total abstinence, but no one denies that it can be a difficult and life-long process. Many doctors believe that a reduction in drug use has to be considered at least a partial success. By this book's definition, drug abuse is causing distress and harm in your life, and a reduction of harm, even if not completely eliminated, is a good thing.

In earlier chapters we saw that drugs overwhelm the brain and produce long-lasting changes in powerful brain systems. From this perspective, it is no wonder that addiction is a serious, chronic, and relapsing disorder, and that recovery can be a difficult, long process with setbacks. Perhaps progress doesn't have to be complete abstinence, but any kind of progress, no matter how little or great, helps. Sometimes just a little progress has to be accepted for now with the hope and expectation of greater progress and abstinence later.

Why Treat Them? They're Only Addicts!

This is an important issue and has to do with society's views and attitudes about addicts. Addicts and addiction carry a stigma. Many consider drug use a moral failing requiring something like an awakening, an epiphany or a spiritual rebirth for a cure. Many feel that addiction is something that the individuals do to themselves so therefore they should undo it by themselves. Why bother with addicts? Let them figure it out! There is a lot of self-righteousness and moralizing in some groups. But research in addiction over the last decades has shown that addiction is a brain-based disorder due to biological and environmental factors. From this perspective, drug abuse is similar to other diseases, such as cardiovascular disease, for example.

Cardiovascular disease usually refers to atherosclerosis, which is a disease of the arteries. Cardiovascular disease is costly to treat because of the expense of medicines and medical procedures, loss of productivity, and the worry of the patients. The cardiovascular patients can be at least partly to blame because they might choose, in many cases, to lead a sedentary lifestyle and continue to eat high fat foods. The patients have at least partial control over the disease in that they can visit their doctor, take medicine, exercise, and watch their diet. One can argue that they voluntarily initiate their disease by improper diet and lack of exercise and perhaps by lack of attention to health care. Treatment is both behavioral and medical. It is behavioral in that they must modify their behavior in accordance with the advice of doctors, counselors, dieticians, and personal trainers. It is medical in that they must take their medicine and regularly see their physician. The doctor might suggest that they need to change their lifestyle by breaking some ingrained, bad habits and by learning and adopting some good ones. Sometimes, in spite of everyone's best efforts, the patient dies. We just don't know enough to cure every cardiovascular patient. But we can prevent or reduce cardiovascular disease in many people.

Drug addiction is similar to cardiovascular disease. The emotional and treatment cost is great. The patients have initiated their disease and are at least partly to blame. They have some control over their behavior, and a lifestyle change is needed. Treatment is both behavioral and medical. Sometimes treatment doesn't improve things and the addicts continue drug use. Perhaps their habits, environmental pressures, inherited traits, and other factors are so strong that we haven't yet found a way to beat them. In spite of the similarity, cardiovascular disease carries much less blame and stigma than addiction. Addicts deserve the same help and attention as anyone with any kind of brain disorder or disease.[1] Unfortunately, many addicts don't want their drug use known. The fear of being stigmatized prevents many from seeking and sticking with treatment. What can we do to help? We can develop a more compassionate and supportive attitude about addiction and treatment, and we *all* can try to combat the stigma of drug addiction. We can think of drug addiction in the same way we think of cardiovascular disease, asthma, or late onset diabetes—as a preventable disorder.

Principles of Treatment

Drug abuse is complex and is the result of many interacting factors (refer to Chapter 8, "Could I Become an Addict?," Figure 8-1, which describes these interacting and additive factors). Accordingly, treatment is geared to meet this complexity. If treatment has not worked for someone, then it might not have been done or understood properly. There are several important, general principles that characterize good treatment. Dr. Martin Adler and his colleagues have summarized principles of effective treatment.[2] Reading through these provides an idea of what to look for in a treatment plan, or why treatment might have failed in some cases.

The *first* principle is that no single treatment is good for all individuals. What a counselor would do for a college student who gets stoned on marijuana a lot, and whose grades are falling is different from what a doctor would do for a sixty-year-old alcoholic who has imbibed every day for years and years and is on the verge of liver failure. Importantly, if treatment does not seem to be working, consider another type or source of treatment. A life might be at stake!

A *second* principle is that adequate treatment must be found. It might be far away and expensive. However, much is at stake and the patient might have to make nearly heroic efforts to get proper care, but, as described, it is worth it. *Third*, effective treatment addresses multiple problems of the person. Because drug use can have multiple roots—including family history, availability, and anxiety or depression—and occurs in a social setting that includes family, a group of friends, a neighborhood, and so on, it is very complex. All of the various parts of this complexity must be addressed to give the drug user the best chance of staying drug free and rehabilitating.

Fourth, treatment plans must be assessed and modified to meet the subject's changing needs. As drug users improve, or even if they get worse, the best treatment might change. For example, after some improvement, the drug user might be ready for vocational training, if suitable. Flexibility in treatment is important and it can offer substantial, new opportunities that drug users haven't had before. *Fifth*, subjects must remain in treatment for an adequate period of time to get benefit. Research suggests that it can take about three months of treatment for the patient to show significant improvement. Too many people give up and leave before they can derive enough benefit. *Sixth*, counseling and "behavioral therapies" should be part of treatment. Drug users often need to rebuild personal and social skills that include problem-solving and succeeding in relationships. Medications can't do this, although they can facilitate them. *Seventh*, medications are important for some users and can be effective when combined with counseling. *Eighth*, drug users with mental problems, such as anxiety or depression, should have access to mental health professionals who can effectively manage and treat mental problems. If a person is taking cocaine to curb his or her depression, getting treatment with counseling and medications such as antidepressants will hopefully eliminate that root need or cause of taking the drug. Again, addiction is a complex disorder.

Ninth, detoxification, or getting the drug out of your system, and coping with withdrawal if necessary, is only the first stage of treatment. By itself, it is unlikely to prevent relapse, but it must be done before the user can move on in treatment. *Tenth*, treatment doesn't have to be voluntary to work. It can be mandated by a judge and data shows that treatment works anyway. It is an urban myth that treatment must be voluntary to succeed. *Eleventh*, drug use must be checked during treatment to assess improvement or relapse. No one expects drug use to stop immediately in all cases, but the status of the patient regarding drugs must be known in order to address it effectively. Relapses or continued drug use are not the end of the world, but they might suggest a different direction of treatment.

The *twelfth* principle is that treatment programs should test for infectious diseases including hepatitis, HIV/AIDS, tuberculosis, and STDs. Instructions on how to avoid health problems can be critical for some users, and overall good health is needed to cope with the stresses of detoxification and treatment. The *last* principle is that recovery from drug use can take a long time and might require multiple episodes of and commitments to treatment. This seems important and the patients—their support groups must appreciate that treatment has to last a long time for many people. Addiction is a relapsing disease or disorder where changes in the brain last a long time.

If you know of a treatment failure, knowledge of these principles might give you some ideas about what went wrong. They might help answer the question "Is there anything else we could have done?"

Do I Want Treatment?

"But I don't have a problem!" This is something that is often heard from individuals who are letting drugs destroy their lives. "I can stop any time I want." This is another thing that is unfortunately sometimes not true. We can easily be in *denial* about ourselves and our problems. Denial frustrates doctors—in itself it is a disease. Having to hit rock bottom and become desperate because of denial is risky and unnecessary. The earlier in life we address drug use and dependence, the more of a productive life we have.

Many drug users misjudge their position, and they don't grasp the benefits of or the need for treatment. It is commonly said that users must hit "rock bottom" before they are shaken into action and seek treatment. Although a crisis can help, it isn't necessary for things to be at an absolute worst before getting help. Many users see where things are headed and decide to get help before a crisis does happen. It can take months of thinking about it before one actually enters treatment. When they do, they are engaged by a professional who has much training and many ideas. The patient must be assessed, and this can involve, depending on the situation, testing—both physical and written, giving a drug history and a personal history. When the situation is understood, a treatment plan can be formulated and treatment begins. Treatment often involves both efforts to modify your behavior and medications that help patients tolerate drug abstinence. But, as has been said before, treatment is flexible and formulated differently to meet the needs of different patients. Therapists have a broad range of techniques and approaches to choose from.

Behavioral Treatments

These treatments focus on behavior and use plans and practices that will modify toxic behavior. Therapy sessions can be individual (one on one) with the counselor, in groups where many patients interact with a trained leader, or in family therapy where family members form the group.

In individual therapy, more time can be devoted to the patient's specific needs. Group therapy, however, can be more economical because six to eight patients might share the cost of the therapist. Also, the more experienced members of the group can be mentors and models for newer patients, and the public nature of the process, where admissions of failures are open, and advice can come from many, can be powerful. Family therapy can be effective when the patient is either at home or have family nearby, and they can be recruited to assist in the treatment process.

Therapies that are proven are available and used in many centers. Although there are too many to summarize, here are some examples that give an idea of what might lie ahead for someone entering treatment. Cognitive Behavioral Therapy, pioneered by Dr. Aaron Beck and others, is designed to help the patient avoid relapse. It is a process where the patients describe high-risk situations, situations where they know they will be weak and perhaps fall back to drug use. Having identified these situations, the patient, along with the therapist, rehearses, role plays, and learns strategies including actions or thoughts that will help him or her survive these high-risk situations. This therapy uses the cognitive or thinking abilities of the patient. It might be especially useful for someone who is intellectually oriented.

Contingency management is another therapy that has been studied by Dr. Steve Higgins and others. It is a technique that uses a reward to divert the patient from dangerous behaviors. Getting the reward is *contingent* or dependent on carrying out specified, helpful behaviors or avoiding destructive behaviors. For example, if a patient has drug-free urine, which is obviously a goal in treatment programs, then he or she might be eligible for a voucher, which has some value. It might be tickets for a movie or credit for a meal. Getting healthy rewards that compete with drug use is effective.

Another treatment is simply exercise. It can be done alone, at one's convenience, and it's free. The Monitoring the Future survey shows that high school students who exercise regularly are less likely to use cigarettes or marijuana than teens who are sedentary.[3] It isn't clear that the effect of exercise is a direct one, but this discovery could have implications for treatment.

Treatment Settings

Treatment is given in different settings and depends on the need of the patient and on the resources that are available. It can be simply given once a week with a school counselor in conjunction with family efforts. It can be given to an inpatient in a hospital or facility specifically designed to treat drug users. It can be given in prison, or it can be mandated by a judge for a non-violent offender as an alternative to prison.

Treatment and prevention can be facilitated in many ways. On March 16, 2011, the *USA Today* newspaper published an article describing how colleges and universities are devoting resources to help students in recovery. Parties in colleges and fraternities are legendary for their supply of drugs and dangerous to someone in recovery. But some students are in treatment and want a place on campus where they can be relatively free of alcohol and other substances and away from the people actively using them. In response to the need, some colleges are establishing drug-free residences and active treatment programs. What a great idea to help young people deal with addictions! After all, young people are among the more vulnerable.

Medications

Medications have proven to be an indispensable part of our repertoire for treatment. They are especially effective when used in conjunction with counseling and behavioral treatments. Because of their importance, there are major research programs aimed at developing newer and better medications. There are useful medications for users of some abused drugs, but not for all. Table 13-1 shows examples of medications for three of the most commonly abused drugs.

TABLE 13-1   Some Medications for Treating Drug Abusers

Addicting Drug	Medication	Comment
Nicotine	bupropion (Zyban)	Used also as an antidepressant.
	varenicline (Chantix)	A "partial agonist" at the nicotine receptor.
	nicotine gum, inhaler,	Objective is nicotine replacement lozenge, or patch to reduce craving and reduce smoking which is harmful.
	clonidine (Catapres)	
Alcohol	disufuram (Antabuse)	Makes one sick when alcohol is taken.
	naltrexone (Depade, ReVia)	Reduces craving for alcohol.
	ondansetron (Zofran)	A serotonin blocker that shows promise.
	topiramate (Topamax)	An anticonvulsant that shows promise.
Opiates (heroin, morphine, oxycontin)	methadone buprenorphine (Subutex, Buprenex)	A maintenance drug.
	naltrexone (Depade, ReVia)	An opiate blocker, also available in long-acting (one month) injectable form.
	nalmefene (Revex)	A long-acting blocker.

Over the years, medications have been developed for helping drug users function in society and become drug free. Some of them are listed in this table. Sometimes combinations of medications are helpful. For example, a recent study revealed that the combination of a nicotine patch plus the nicotine lozenge gave a high success rate for smokers (Piper M.E. et al. A Randomized Placebo-Controlled Clinical Trial of 5 Smoking Cessation Pharmacotherapies. *Arch Gen Psychiatry*, 66:1254-1262, 2009).

Some medications are substitutes, which mean that they act in the same way as the abused substance and reduce craving. Others are blockers, which prevent the abused drugs from having an effect. And yet others act in ways that aren't fully understood but might modify brain circuits involved with reward and addiction. An example of the latter type is naltrexone, which is an *opiate* blocker, but yet is very helpful in reducing *alcohol* intake. For example, one study showed that after 60 days of treatment, 60 percent of those taking naltrexone had not relapsed to alcohol use whereas only 20 percent of those taking a sugar pill had not relapsed.[4] In any case, it is useful that we have different kinds of medications because some individuals might have bad reactions to certain medications.

A controversy usually surrounds the use of substitute medications like methadone, because their use is "just substituting one drug for another." For example, it can be said that methadone is an opiate drug and using it in treatment is simply creating dependence on a different opiate. There is a black market for methadone (and other prescription opiates) where it is sold to active addicts for getting high, and this supports the idea that substitutes are problematic. Similarly, the nicotine patch still gives the user nicotine. The criticism is: what good can substitutes do? The addict is still an addict. This is an important question and confounds people at many levels in society—individuals, law enforcers, and legislators.

There are several ways to look at this controversy. One goal of treatment is to get the addict off the drug, which unfortunately can produce withdrawal. Any way that we can make withdrawal from drug use easier is helpful. Using substitutes in the short term can reduce craving and withdrawal, and gives the addicts time so that they can break up old toxic habits and behavioral patterns. They can also reduce harm and hazard to the user. For example, using nicotine gum or a patch eliminates craving for smoking, which is toxic to the lungs. Another example is the use of oral methadone for IV drug users. Intravenous heroin users are susceptible to a variety of problems including dirty and infectious needles and ignorance of what exactly is injected. Methadone administered orally by a reliable source eliminates those threats. Another practical help is that an approved substitute medication is not illegal; this eliminates the threat of breaking the law, which is confounding and adds yet another problem to the drug problem.

There are other, somewhat more complex, advantages to some substitutes in that they might have different time courses of action, which can be helpful. For example, substitute medications that have a long life in the blood can keep the users more stable than drugs whose blood levels rise and fall rapidly. It must be emphasized that treatment with substitute medications such as methadone works effectively in that addicts stabilized on methadone are more healthy, sociable, and stable, and can hold down a job. Some individuals have been on methadone for decades without any severe side effects. From these perspectives, substitute medications are just fine. Is the problem the medication or is it the way we think about it?

Is Addiction a Metabolic Disease?

In spite of these advantages, many still feel that substitutes are not the answer, or that they are short-term solutions at best. Can we justify long-term use of substitutes like methadone in methadone-maintenance programs? Most knowledgeable people say that methadone-maintenance is helpful, and this might be an example of where we need to challenge our traditional thinking about the evil of substitutes. In the 1960s, Drs. Vincent Dole and Marie Nyswander saw that addicts compulsively sought out heroin as though they really needed it to function normally. Said another way, drug addiction can be like diabetes in that diabetics require an external source of insulin, which is deficient or not working properly in the bodies of diabetics. This is the notion that addicts, even though perhaps a small fraction of our total population, are seeking to correct a metabolic deficiency in their brains by taking drugs. Dole and Nyswander examined the idea and selected methadone for testing because it was active when taken by mouth, lasted 24 hours, and was reasonably nontoxic. They found that opiate addicts did stabilize on methadone and stopped their out-of-control search for drugs.[5] The drug users were able to focus on rehabilitation because they weren't distracted and driven by their drug-deficient brains. These results have been confirmed in thousands of centers and trials, and methadone-maintenance has been a great success medically and socially. Patients maintained on methadone do not appear any different from others, and the courts have established that patients may not be barred from any kind of employment solely because they are taking methadone. From this perspective, our attitudes and the stigma we put on drug abuse is the problem, not the use of substitutes. It will be interesting to see how the thinking of our society evolves on this topic.

Best Treatment Is Prevention

Prevention includes the policies and actions taken to prevent new or continuing drug abuse in a target population. If we can prevent the non-drug-using population from becoming drug users, then we can greatly reduce the burden of drug abuse. The idea is to prevent the damage before it occurs. Anti-tobacco and antidrug advertising are examples of prevention efforts. Prevention works! For example, two educational programs in schools, Life Skills Training (LST) and the Strengthening Families Program (SFP),[6] that are aimed at prevention of drug use have reduced marijuana smoking and alcohol use. The cost of these programs can be just one tenth of a year of outpatient treatment. The youth of this country are not stupid. When told about the problems with drugs, many listen. Figure 13-1 shows a reduction in drug use by youths after being told about the dangers of drugs.

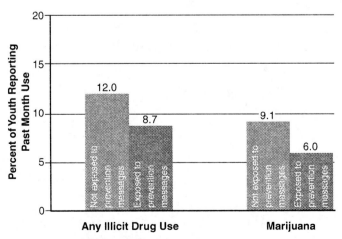

Figure 13-1 Providing information about the dangers of drug use to adolescents reduces drug use. (From NSDUH, SAMHSA, September 2008, and http://www.whitehousedrugpolicy.gov/mediacampaign/about.html, accessed March 23, 2011.)

How Does Someone Get Help?

A young drug addict has been surveying his life. He is in his early thir-
ties, has lost his job and family, some of his health, and almost all of
his wealth. His family and friends barely talk to him, and he doesn't
seem to have anywhere to go. He knows it can still get worse, but he
makes a decision to get help. Where does he start?

There are several ways to find help. Family doctors are likely to
know how to help, or at least how to begin. There are also several kinds
of professionals that specialize in treating drug abusers. This group is
the top of the heap in that they have the special training that it takes to
assess and address drug problems. School counselors and clergy usually
can be counted on to be knowledgeable and keep conversations confi-
dential. They are often among the first to notice drug problems. School
officials, in particular, who observe students' performance, often know
whether someone is having problems, and they try to help.

Although friends and family are not professionals, they often play
a critical role in the search for help. They can offer emotional support, and sometimes practical help such as making phone calls or
making some financial commitment to treatment. They are more
likely to be committed to someone's well-being than strangers.
Moreover, they know the person well and might have insights to the
problem, which might be due to a circle of drug-using acquaintances,
or an illness, and so on. But family and friends might be an excellent
place to start. Maybe someone who is in treatment can be a guide.
Maybe they can sponsor friends in Alcoholics Anonymous meetings
or in Narcotics Anonymous, if relevant. If someone can't find help
through friends and family, or if they make it worse, like assuming the
drug user is an irretrievable failure, then they should move on. Go
elsewhere to get help.

It is also possible to get information and even find help through
the Internet. For example, the National Institute on Drug Abuse
(NIDA) and the Substance Abuse and Mental Health Services
Administration (SAMHSA) have informative websites. Table 13-2

lists many websites that were found in a recent search and includes some relevant comments about them. These organizations have people who are willing to assist people seeking treatment. Some are connected to a specific facility, and some offer to find treatment in the area where the patient lives. There are private programs where the patient pays either out of pocket, with insurance, or both, and there are free or low-cost programs such as state-funded programs. Note that the last entries are for sexual addiction. It is advisable to check the credentials and qualifications of any caregiver or professional. It is possible that some potential caregivers are bogus or misguided.

TABLE 13-2   Websites Offering Help

Website or Address	Phone Number	Comment
http://dasis3.samhsa.gov/	(none given)	Helps you locate a treatment center based on your location
http://www.aa.org/lang/en/meeting_finder.cfm?origpage=29	(none given) Anonymous meeting	Helps you find an Alcoholics
http://www.na.org/?ID=phoneline	(none given)	Helps you find a Narcotics Anonymous meeting
Drug-Rehab.org	1 877 392 5926	Helps you find local help
Turntohelp.com	1 866 973 4373	Focuses on opiate dependence. Directs to an MD and a "coach"
www.help.addicted.org	(none given)	Provides directions to local and low-cost treatment
http://www.recoveryconnection.org/	1 800 993 3869	Refers to treatment in state of Florida
Kidshealth.org	(none given)	Focuses on children and teens—helpful to parents
http://www.drugfree.org/intervene	(none given)	For teens with problems—helpful to parents
Spiritualriver.com	(none given)	Information on how to help someone in trouble with drugs

TABLE 13-2   Websites Offering Help

Website or Address	Phone Number	Comment
http://www.addict-help.com/	(none given)	A general resource
http://www.teen-drug-abuse.org/	1 866 323 5611	Inpatient and outdoor programs for teens
http://www.addictionhelp services.com/get-help.asp	1 877 554 7308	Offers guidance
Helpguide.org	(not given)	Offers general assistance
http://www.sexual-addiction.net/	1 888 762 3753	For sexual addiction, an inpatient private facility.
http://www.sash.net/en/ find-a therapist.html	1 706 356 7031	Helps you locate a therapist

There are many sources of help and many ways to find help; however, be sure the caregivers are qualified.

Summary

Drug abuse is a brain-based disorder like so many other illnesses such as anxiety and depression. Treatment, by qualified caregivers, is the solution for drug abuse and addiction. It is an ongoing, long-lasting *process,* rather than a specific event with an end. It actually saves money in addition to reducing misery. Substitute medications such as methadone are effective and successful. A barrier to treatment is the stigma associated with being a drug user, and the stigma must be overcome. Every person in this country can help by adjusting his or her own attitudes, and by helping others become more tolerant of and knowledgeable about addiction. The characteristics and components of good treatment are known. Preventing drug use from getting started is especially effective and an important goal for society.

Endnotes

[1] McLellan, A.T., Lewis, D.C., O'Brien, C.P. and Kleber, H.D.. "Drug Dependence, A Chronic Medical Illness." *JAMA* 284(13): 1689–1695, 2000. This is an example of a paper that describes drug abuse as a brain disorder deserving of routine standard medical care. It compares drug abuse to other chronic diseases including hypertension, asthma, and type 2 diabetes mellitus, and it finds similarities.

[2] Summarized from Adler M. et al. "The Treatment of Drug Addiction: a Review." In Graham et al, *Principles of Addiction Medicine*, Third edition, American Society of Addiction Medicine, p 419, 2003. The principles are also summarized from *Principles of Drug Addiction Treatment: A Research Based Guide*. Rockville MD: NIDA, Chapter 2, NIH Publication No. 99-4180. The wording of the second principle was changed slightly to make it a more positive statement.

[3] See the article "Lower Rates of Cigarette and Marijuana Smoking Among Exercising Teens." *NIDA Notes*, 22(4): 20, 2009.

[4] O'Malley S.S. et al. "Naltrexone and Coping Skills Therapy for Alcohol Dependence." *Arch Gen Psychiatry*, 49: 881–887, 1992.

[5] Dole, V.P. "Implications of Methadone Maintenance for Theories of Narcotic Addiction." *JAMA*, 260: 3025–3029, 1988. In this paper, Vincent Dole describes his work and experiences in the context of a receptor theory. This work is some of the most important in all of drug addiction research.

[6] For example, Spoth R.L. et al. "Longitudinal Substance Initiation Outcomes for a Universal Preventive Intervention Combining Family and School Programs." *Psychol Addict Behav*, 16: 129–134, 2002.

14

What Does the Future Hold?

There are many themes in this book. One is that a drug addict is someone who has lost (at least some) control over his or her ability to seek and take drugs, and this loss of control leads to distress and problems for the drug user. Almost all drugs that humans abuse are also self-administered by animals, suggesting that drug taking is an innate drive that is widespread in many species. Moreover, many studies show that drug taking is involved with specific physiological systems in the brain. Because drug taking adversely alters brain chemistry, we can develop medications to reverse these negative changes; in fact, many useful medications have already been developed. Drug abuse produces long-lasting (months to years) changes in the brain, suggesting that these changes are the basis of the chronic and relapsing nature of drug addiction. Abstaining from drugs for a week or a month after long-term use is probably not enough time for the brain to return to normal and heal. The injury to the vulnerable brain increases the drive to take drugs. Drugs act through powerful systems in the brain, systems that have evolved to ensure the survival of our species. Drugs gain control of these natural systems and cause unnatural adaptations and effects. It is believed these factors, taken together, form the basis of drug addiction, a brain disorder or disease. Although many people can walk away from drugs on their own, many can't. Some individuals are more vulnerable than others, and, realizing that they need help, seek professional treatment. Treatment for drug abuse is effective when done either voluntarily or by mandate, and it is geared to the specific needs of the individual. Great progress has been made in this field, and more is needed. But, where is all this taking us? What does the future hold?

Treatment, Treatment, Treatment

Many treatment providers feel that it would be wonderful if we could get what we already know about drug abuse into greater use. Public health would be served greatly if drug abuse prevention and treatment were integrated into primary care across the country. It would mean that a routine visit to the doctor would include screening, treatment if needed, and referrals as part of primary care. It sounds simple, but perhaps the stigma of drug addiction is part of the problem.

New and better treatments are also needed to reduce the costly burden of addiction in our society, and the cost is measured not only in money but also in misery. Studies of various treatments and treatment programs will reveal what is most effective in treatment, and these practices will be adopted by other programs. This approach works, but it will take time, money, and support. New medications are needed and will undoubtedly help in this effort. Although there are government-approved and medically accepted medications for treating smoking and alcohol abuse, there are none for treating psychostimulant abuse. Clearly, there are some gaps in addiction treatment that must be filled. Also, medications with fewer side effects are needed. In general, improvement in the treatment of drug abuse, one of our most costly disorders or diseases, is essential.

Prevention, which includes education of the public about drugs, is also effective, and more and better preventive measures are needed. As with treatment, studies of prevention will reveal the best prevention methods. Studies of vulnerability will reveal which groups are the most likely to abuse certain drugs, and these are the groups that can be targeted by improved prevention techniques.

Molecules of Addiction

Drugs produce changes in the brain, and these changes are in the levels and activity of various molecules in certain neurons. For example, drugs seem to reduce the levels of D2 dopamine receptors, which have been discussed previously. These and other changes form the cellular and molecular bases of addictive behavior. Therefore, knowledge of these molecular events is critical for understanding drug addiction. Understanding a disease does not necessarily mean we can cure it, but it at least defines the problem. This understanding also sets the stage for a possible cure when new techniques and approaches develop over time.

The story of dopamine has been told to illustrate how brain chemicals mediate addiction. But dopamine is not the only important neurotransmitter. We have mentioned others including glutamate, GABA, serotonin, enkephalins, and anandamide. Addiction is complex and involves systems and circuits of neurons with many neurotransmitters. In the future, we hope to better specify the neurotransmitters and the specific neurons that are critical for addiction. We have made progress on this, but more remains to be done. In addition to neurotransmitters, a number of larger molecules such as proteins (transporters, receptors, and so on) are important for addiction. Again, we have learned much but much remains to be discovered.

As detailed in previous chapters, we know something about the genes involved in addiction, and we know something about the various molecules that are involved as well. We are learning about the important new science, epigenetics, and how drugs cause epigenetic changes in gene expression. As described in Chapter 5, "The Dark Side Develops!," epigenetic changes in neurons in the brain change the levels of various proteins in the nerve cells, such as the mesolimbic neurons. We know a little bit about the drug-induced changes in gene expression and various molecules. But this knowledge needs to be extended and refined. Significant advances are likely in this area in the future. Someday, this knowledge will be translated into gains in new medications and treatments.

Vaccines

Vaccines are major public health tools that are responsible for the eradication of smallpox, the prevention of childhood diseases, and the control of many injurious illnesses. Treatment with a vaccine results in the development of antibodies specific for some target, known as an antigen. The antigen can be a virus, for example, but it is really a protein that is part of the virus. When the antibody binds to the protein on the virus, the virus is prevented from infecting the cells of the vaccinated host. Antibody molecules are Y-shaped proteins that bind to the antigen at the tip of the two arms of the Y. The binding is highly specific for the antigen in the vaccine, and the antibody can be thought of as a specific deactivator or blocker. Although we most often think of antibodies as protecting us against infectious diseases, antibodies can also be made against specific drug molecules.

In 1973, Drs. B. Wainer, F. Fitch, R. Rothberg, and C.R. Schuster published a paper in *Nature* showing that antibodies against morphine blocked the action of morphine on a functioning, contracting tissue.[1] Traditionally, antibodies are made against large molecules like proteins, and the generation of effective antibodies against a small molecule like morphine was a significant achievement. Not only were the antibodies produced, they were active in that they bound morphine and prevented morphine from having a biological effect. A simple analogy is restraining someone from reaching and doing something injurious to another person. The antibody binds and restrains the molecule so that it can't do anything. From this seminal study, the idea of producing vaccinations against addicting drugs took hold. For example, it has been shown that vaccinating someone with a protein that has many cocaine molecules attached to it can result in the body producing antibodies against cocaine. The antibody is in the blood of the vaccinated individual (see Figure 14-1). It has been shown that this vaccination procedure is effective in reducing the behavioral effects produced by cocaine. Vaccines against addicting drugs (cocaine, nicotine, phencyclidine [PCP], and methamphetamine) are not yet routinely available but are currently in development. In clinical trials, these vaccines have been effective and shown promise. For example, in a recent study of the cocaine vaccine, the patients that produced the most antibodies against cocaine used less of this drug, presumably because they experienced little reward from taking cocaine. Without these rewarding effects, the act of taking the drug is not reinforced. It will be important to develop better vaccines and procedures that maximize the benefits of this therapeutic approach.

The idea of using vaccines to treat drug abusers has some important, novel aspects. To see this more clearly, let us look at more traditional, non-vaccine treatment medications, such as methadone or naltrexone, which are used to treat opiate addicts. These medications are both active but in different ways. The first one stimulates opiate receptors and the second one blocks them. In both cases, the medication is doing something to the brain's process of neurotransmission, and these medications have to get into the brain to work. Although in the brain, they produce useful changes that benefit the drug user. However, they are also having other effects—side effects[2] that can't be avoided. For example, long-term use of methadone can result in changes in blood proteins and prolactin—and there is still the danger of overdose. *All* of the drugs used in psychiatry have to get into the brain to work, and they all have at least some side effects and dangers. But, and this is the interesting part, antibodies don't get into the brain. They don't have to. They don't do anything to neurotransmission. Rather, they reside in the blood and prevent the dangerous drugs from getting into the brain. In the clinical trial mentioned at the end of the last paragraph, the antibodies against cocaine prevented the drug from entering the brain and thus prevented the drug-induced reward. Without a reward, there is no incentive to take the drug. The use of vaccines to treat drug abuse will be an interesting adventure in treatment. It is a new approach, but will it be useful in the long run, or will prohibitive problems develop? We can only try it, and wait and see. But everyone is hopeful.

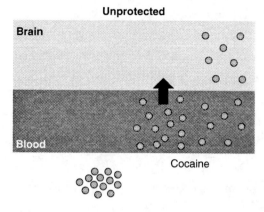

Figure 14-1 Antibodies prevent drugs from entering the brain. Consider the
top half of the diagram. There are four frames from left to right showing the
sequence for a drug. In the left frame, there are no cocaine molecules (circles)
and the blood and brain compartments are shown without drug. The next
frame shows cocaine entering the blood, the third frame shows cocaine in the
blood about to enter the brain, and the fourth frame shows cocaine diffusing
from the blood into the brain where it will produce its effects. Now examine the
lower half of the diagram. In the left frame, the blood has antibodies, either
from vaccination or from direct injection. The second frame shows antibodies
going into the blood (Y-shaped molecules) and cocaine entering the blood
either from ingestion or injection. The third frame shows the critical event—the
antibodies bind to the cocaine in the blood so that the drug cannot get into the
brain, or only a small amount gets in as shown in the fourth frame. In the case
of vaccines, the patient's immune system has been recruited to produce an
antibody that prevents or reduces cocaine's effects. Dr. Thomas Kosten, his
colleagues and others have been carrying out this work. (From Whitten, L.
"Cocaine Vaccine Helps Reduce Drug Use." NIDA Notes, Vol. 23, December
2010.)

RTI-336

As we have seen, new medications are needed. Because there are no medications for psychostimulant (including cocaine, amphetamine, and methamphetamine) addicts, this is one area where help is important. As an example, let us consider one possible candidate for a medication, RTI-336.[3] For the sake of discussion, let us look at it as a medication for cocaine users, although it can be used for any psychostimulant drug (see Figure 14-2).

RTI-336 is the result of an effort of a diverse group of scientists with complementary skills who were searching for a substitute medication for cocaine.[4] What are the properties that we would want in such a medication? *First*, it should be less toxic than cocaine. Cocaine acts at many sites in the brain, and a medication that acts only at the *addicting* site for cocaine would be desirable so that other unrelated actions (side effects) would be avoided.[5] *Next*, cocaine gets into the brain quickly and, depending on how it is taken, can impart the much sought after "rush" of feelings that addicts like. A medication is best if it enters the brain more slowly so as to be less emotionally disruptive and less addicting. (It is thought that drugs entering the brain quickly are more addicting than those entering more slowly.) Cocaine's duration of action is about one and half hours, which is short and is presumably why cocaine users binge, or repeatedly take the drug over a several hour period. A medication should have a longer duration of action so as to have a continued therapeutic effect and so that it doesn't have to be taken often. Medications that have to be taken often are less successful because people forget to take them as often as needed. Finally, a realistic laboratory test is that an injection of the candidate medication into an animal that is self-administering cocaine should produce a reduction in cocaine self-administration.

It turns out that RTI-336 (see Figure 14-2) is an ideal medication candidate for many reasons. It is selective for the dopamine transporter, which is responsible for the addicting properties of cocaine, it enters the brain more slowly than cocaine, and it has a duration of action that is longer than cocaine's. In addition, it reduces the self-administration of cocaine by animals after injection. Preclinical toxicity studies show that RTI-336 has very little toxicity, and in early phase human clinical trials it also had low toxicity. But, more clinical trials with drug users are needed to show that it works effectively in psychostimulant addicts.

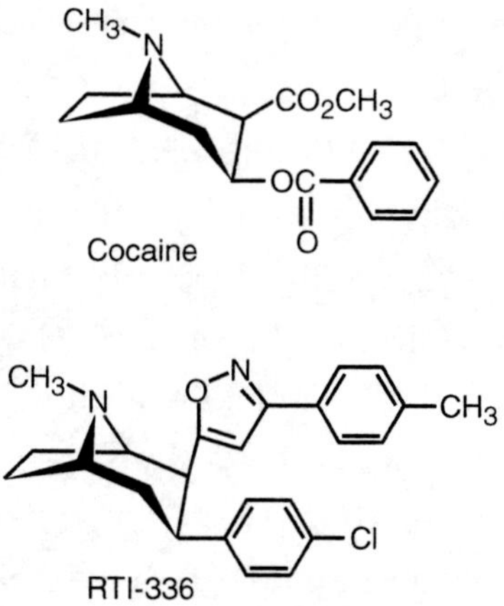

Figure 14-2   Chemical structure of cocaine and RTI-336. One can see at a glance that RTI-336 and cocaine are similar in some ways and different in others. The similarity of the two is why RTI-336 acts like cocaine and can be a substitute medication for the drug. The differences, however, are key. RTI-336 is more specific and selective acting than cocaine, gets into the brain more slowly, and seems to lack prohibitive toxicity. The compound was synthesized by Dr. Ivy Carroll and colleagues at the Research Triangle Institute (RTI). (The drawing was provided by Dr. Ivy Carroll.)

Are there drawbacks or concerns? Yes, as there is with every new, potential medication. Will previously unknown side effects be discovered? Will it continue to be effective or will tolerance develop? Will the fact that it is a substitute medication[6] create controversy? These are issues that must be considered by regulatory agencies and doctors with any and every new medication candidate.

Stigma of Being a Druggie!

Drug use and addiction are stigmatized. It means that drug users are often looked down upon, and not seen as fully equal or acceptable to us. They are seen as perhaps less than fully functional or capable. Would we consider them for a job that was important to us? We would worry about their reliability and their performance. We know their problem is long lasting and we would wonder how long is long enough without relapse. When they have a prison record related to drugs, many feel that that is just too much—they are stigmatized even further.

Drug users are usually aware of all this, and they might think about these issues themselves. This can contribute to self-loathing, adding a self-esteem problem to an already huge drug problem. Their motivation is blunted: "Why should I finish school? They won't give me a job anyway with my police record." Having tried to stop using drugs only to relapse, they might lack confidence in their ability to stop using. They might feel trapped and truly hopeless. Some would rather use drugs than face the stigma of being labeled as an addict— why deal with that? Because drug use is sometimes more or less secret, going into treatment is akin to making it public and official. If seeking treatment creates more trouble for users, they might prefer to deal with the drug use on their own. Families that normally help out when an illness occurs might go into denial or be afraid of stigmatizing themselves or everyone in the family when the illness is drug addiction. Overall, the stigma can be debilitating.

But the world has many recovered addicts, and recovery *is* possible. It is possible to stop using drugs and begin to lead a normal life. Sometimes it is a long road, so it is best to start as soon as possible. There are many who are willing to help recovering addicts and they can make a big difference. Because there are many ways of helping, people need to be available and attuned to the possibilities. Because of the fear of stigmatization, discretion is vital in any helper. A supportive conversation, or suggestions on how to get help, can be done best with a promise of discretion. But we all need to look at and into ourselves—can we accept recovering drug users? Can we extend ourselves to help them and put aside our own judgments? These things are necessary for them and for us.

Legalization or Decriminalization

The illicit drug problem is a frustrating one. Trying to stop illicit drugs from entering our country, or from being made here, has not been successful. There are highly publicized victories in the form of seizures of drugs or military victories in source countries—but the problem continues. Drug addicts continue using these drugs in spite of the serious problems they cause, and drug-related crime has far from gone away. Addicts and their families complain about the illegal status of many drugs because it compounds the problem. For example, just the possession of a drug can be illegal and result in expensive litigation or confinement. These can interfere with finding appropriate treatment. Under these kinds of circumstances, helping an arrested addict can even create legal risks for the helpers. For these reasons, many people have proposed that some illegal drugs be legalized. It is claimed that this would reduce the prices of these drugs, perhaps provide revenue through taxation, reduce society's costs of law enforcement, and save drug users from the additional stigma of breaking the law. A prison record can be a significant hindrance to full recovery and working in society. Legalization sounds interesting and good to some, but is it really a good idea?

If we view drug abuse solely as a criminal or legal problem, then legalization would be a focus and could be discussed, although it is not simple by any means. But, drug abuse is a *different* problem; it is a brain disorder, and in this sense legalization will not help, but, in fact, will likely make drug use worse. The reason it will make it worse is because legalization will increase the availability of drugs. If drugs are more readily available, then there will be more people dependent on drugs, and that dependence is well known to create problems for users. Some straightforward evidence for this was shown in Figure 1-1 and its legend. The legal drugs, alcohol and nicotine, are much more widely and frequently used than the illegal drugs by maybe a factor of ten. Imagine what would happen if the illicit drugs were made legal. Heroin, cocaine, and amphetamine are not less addicting than alcohol and nicotine. A public health perspective says that legalization, as a blanket, unrestricted policy, will not help but will most likely hurt because there will be more drug users. But, it is possible that reductions in some penalties (decriminalization) could be useful in some cases. There is a difference between legalization and decriminalization.

On June 17, 2011, the 40th anniversary of the "war on drugs," President Jimmy Carter wrote an op-ed piece in the *New York Times* (p. A31) entitled "Call off the Global Drug War." He cites surveys showing that the "war" has failed. In the last ten years, drug consumption has significantly increased: 34.5 percent for opiates, 27 percent for cocaine, and 8.5 percent for cannabis. Moreover, current policies have contributed to the burgeoning prison population in this country—more than 3 percent of American adults are either in prison, on probation, or on parole! This is a higher proportion than any other industrialized country. The "war on drugs" seems more harmful than the drug problem itself. He notes that the Global Commission on Drug Policy recommends that the focus on low-level, non-violent drug users should be deemphasized, and international, violent criminal organizations should be targeted. Treatment should be the focus for the average drug user.

Dr. Avram Goldstein, a leader in the field of drug addiction, thinks that neither total prohibition nor total legalization are good ideas, and that each drug is unique and requires its own consideration and level of control.[7] He has made a number of suggestions. Tobacco and alcohol are too readily available and a variety of steps could be taken to reduce their availability. Opiate drugs such as heroin and psychostimulants (for example, cocaine) are currently regulated and they should remain so because they are dangerous. Marijuana is not harmless, but perhaps some penalties associated with its use and possession could be reduced. Other drugs like inhalants are toxic and are used often by children; they need to be targeted for abuse prevention. Many of these ideas have been discussed among public health professionals, and their implementation has been tried in various ways. Dr. Griffith Edwards, an expert from the UK, has also commented on the alcohol problem and has made relatively similar suggestions.[8] In any case, drug addiction is a serious illness with many consequences for the user, and any policy or action must take this into account.

What Should Our Attitude Be and How Can We Help?

Some reasonable recommendations[9] for combating drug abuse are as follows. Treat drug abuse as a public health problem and support reducing drug use by treatment and prevention education. (This is not saying that drug users who break the law should not be held accountable.) Focus on the collateral damage caused by drugs. This includes the spread of infectious diseases such as HIV and STDs because of bad health practices and poor judgment due to drug use. Support prevention efforts because they are the least expensive way to reduce the costs of drug abuse to society. Prevent use in children, because people who do not use drugs from ages 10 to 20 years of age are unlikely to start using drugs in later life. Support increasing funding for research into the process of addiction, treatment, prevention, and drug policies. Finally, help prevent the stigmatization of drug abusers so that they can more readily get help.

Summary

Lessons from history suggest that drug abuse, in some form and way, will be with us in the future, even though it is destructive to the drug user and society. Accordingly, understanding this brain disorder and improving treatment and prevention are essential. This requires continued public support for additional research and treatment, and a steady effort against the counterproductive stigma of this illness.

Endnotes

[1] Wainer, B.H., Fitch, F.W., Rothberg, R.M., C.R. Schuster. "In Vitro Morphine Antagonism by Antibodies." *Nature*, February 23; 241(5391): 537–538, 1973.

[2] Every single medication that we use has side effects at some dose. Aspirin can cause stomach bleeding. Some antidepressants can cause a reduced sex drive. Some antibiotics cause diarrhea. Doctors are trained to know this and to evaluate if the risk to the patient is worthwhile. The risk to benefit ratio is an important consideration for every medication.

[3] I, the author, was the leader of the early testing team. The synthetic chemistry leader was Dr. F. Ivy Carroll, and Dr. Leonard Howell carried out the self-administration testing. I also disclose that I am one of the developers of RTI-336 and co-share a patent on it. Relevant publications include:

> Carroll, F. I., Pawlush, N, Kuhar, M.J., Pollard, G.T., and Howard, J.L.. "Synthesis, Monoamine Transporter Binding Properties, and Behavioral Pharmacology of a Series of 3, -(Substituted Phenyl)-2, -(3'-substituted Isoxazol-5-yl)tropanes," *J Med Chemistry*, 47 (2): 296–302, 2004.

> Carroll, F.I., Howard, J.L., Howell, L.L., Fox, B.S., and Kuhar, M.J. "Development of the Dopamine Transporter Selective RTI-336 as a Pharmacotherapy for Cocaine Abuse." *AAPS Journal*, 8(1): E196–E203, 2006.

[4] Ibid.

[5] The addicting site of action for cocaine is the dopamine transporter, and cocaine blocks the transporter. Cocaine thereby increases the level of dopamine in the synapse and enhances dopaminergic neurotransmission. See also Figure 4-4 and Figure 11-4 from Chapters 4 and 11, respectively.

[6] Substitute medications have been discussed in Chapter 12, "Women and Adolescents." Successful substitutes are the nicotine patch and methadone, for nicotine and opiate addicts, respectively. Substitute medications for cocaine, for example, would act in the same manner as cocaine but have other properties that make the medications helpful.

[7] Goldstein, A. *Addiction: From Biology to Drug Policy*, Second edition. New York: Oxford University Press, p 293, 2001.

[8] Dr. Griffith Edwards has commented on alcohol and the public good in publications such as: Edwards, G. "Alcohol policy and the public good." *Addiction*, 92 (Suppl 1): S73-9, 1997; Edwards, G. "The Trouble with Drink: Why Ideas Matter." *Addiction*, 105: 797–804, 2010.

[9] More complete policy recommendations of several groups are as follows. See endnotes numbered 7 and 8, the NIDA strategic plan, NIH publication Number 10-6119, published September 2010, SAMHSA strategic plan at http://www.samhsa.gov/about/SAMHSAStrategicPlan.pdf. Accessed July 11, 2011.

Glossary

acetylcholine A chemical compound. A neurotransmitter found in the brain and at the nerve-muscle junction.

action potential An electrical impulse that moves down an axon and causes a release of neurotransmitter from the nerve terminal. A change in the electrical membrane potential of a cell that is necessary for communication between cells.

addict Someone dependent on drugs for maintaining functioning and or a state of well being. The DSM IV TR has the official definition of a variety of states of drug use.

adrenal gland Attached to the top of the kidneys, it participates in the stress response by releasing cortisol and other compounds.

amygdala A structure located deep within the brain; it is known to play a role in emotional memory and fear.

anterior cingulate gyrus A part of the cerebral cortex associated with important cognitive functions such as error detection, empathy, and expectation of rewards.

antibody Specifically shaped proteins derived from the immune system that help bind and immobilize foreign proteins such as those in viruses and bacteria.

antigen A molecule that can trigger an immune response and the production of a specific antibody against the antigen.

axon The cellular extension from a nerve cell body that carries the action potential or impulse and ends in nerve terminals.

behavioral therapy   A therapy for treating drug abusers that focuses on a patient's behaviors or actions.

CART peptide   A neuropeptide and neurotransmitter that acts in many regions of the brain and is believed to play a role in eating, stress, and reward.

cerebral cortex   The newest and most highly evolved part of the forebrain that is thought to embody our ability for language, cognition, memory, and sensory-motor perception.

chromosomes   A specific arrangement of DNA and proteins found in the nuclei of cells that contains the genes.

cortisol   A steroid hormone derived from the adrenal gland that is released to carry out a variety of metabolic actions in response to stress.

cue   Anything associated with drug use that, when experienced, can reinstate drug use after abstinence.

decriminalization   The process of removing or reducing criminal penalties for drug-related offenses.

dendrite   The input region of a neuron that extends from a neuronal cell body and receives nerve terminals and synapses from other neurons.

Diagnostic and Statistical Manual of Mental Disorders (DSM)   Published through the American Psychiatric Association, the current version is the DSM IV TR. It provides descriptions and codes for diagnosis of mental disorders and includes substance use disorders.

DNA   A nucleic acid consisting of an organism's genetic material and found in the chromosomes.

dopamine   A neurotransmitter that is commonly recognized for its role in reward and reinforcement.

drug   In this book, a substance ingested that produces reward and reinforcement and that may produce a state of addiction.

drug abuse   Use of a drug to the point where it provides no benefit and endangers the user because of side effects or addiction. It is also described as a maladaptive pattern of drug use.

drug self-administration   Procedure where a drug is taken by a subject who controls the process. This important procedure can define if a drug has the potential to be addicting, as most drugs that humans abuse are self-administered by animals.

Electrical Self-Stimulation (ESS)   Procedure whereby stimulation of an electrode in certain brain regions is rewarding and reinforcing and is maintained by the subject who has control over the process.

epigenetics   The study of nongenetic influences or mechanisms without changes in the sequence of DNA that result in changes in an organism's gene expression. The mechanisms usually involve methylation of DNA or changes in histones that change the access to DNA.

extinction   In animal studies, the period where a drug is withheld and the drug-seeking behavior eventually stops.

gene   Hereditary segments of DNA that code for proteins.

gene expression   A process where genes are translated into mRNA and then proteins.

gene variant   A gene with minor mutation in an organism that is different from the same gene in another organism.

genetic mutation   An alteration in the chemical makeup of a gene that most likely leads to altered gene expression or an altered protein. Although these may cause serious disease, it is also possible that no functional consequences come about from a mutation.

hypothalamus   A structure located deep within the brain with numerous homeostatic functions that are essential to survival, such as feeding, sex, and sleep. It is responsible for controlling autonomic and endocrine systems.

in vitro   Studies performed in the laboratory on a biological tissue that has been extracted from the intact organism.

legalization Process of legalizing drug use.

limbic system A network of brain structures responsible for reward, reinforcement, emotion, memory, and olfaction.

medial forebrain bundle A brain area that is part of the reward system and contains fibers connecting the ventral tegmental area and nucleus accumbens.

medication A substance or therapeutic drug that is useful in treating disease.

mesolimbic system A dopaminergic pathway that is commonly associated with reward that extends from the midbrain to the forebrain limbic system.

mRNA Messenger RNA. It is transcribed from a sequence of DNA that ultimately gets translated into proteins.

neuron A brain cell consisting of an axon with nerve terminals, dendrite, and cell body.

neuronal circuit A network of different brain regions coordinating together to carry out a particular function. A series of connected neurons.

neurotransmitter A chemical messenger that allows communication between neurons.

norepinephrine A hormone and neurotransmitter that performs a variety of functions.

nucleus The organelle in eukaryotic cells that contains genetic material. Also, a brain region distinguished by its organization and placement.

nucleus accumbens A brain structure known for its role in reward and reinforcement.

orbitofrontal cortex Part of the frontal, cerebral cortex that is associated with emotions, reward, and decision making.

perinatal Around the time of birth.

PET scan A scan produced by positron emission tomography. It is an imaging technique that uses a radioactive tracer to examine how organs in the body are functioning or to look at the levels of various proteins such as receptors.

phosphorylation A molecular process where a phosphate group is added to an organic molecule, most commonly a protein, to alter or modify its function.

pituitary gland An endocrine gland at the base of the brain responsible for producing many of the bodily hormones.

plasticity An important process whereby experience alters one's neuronal chemistry, structure, or function, resulting in a change in neuronal circuits. It is thought to be the basis of processes such as memory and drug addiction.

promoter A region of a gene responsible for regulating its expression.

protein turnover The process whereby a protein is synthesized, broken down, and replaced.

receptor A protein that is specifically shaped to bind and receive a neurotransmitter molecule. After binding the neurotransmitter, a change takes place such that the receptor mediates another kind of change, either a metabolic or ionic one. Receptors take a chemical signal (neurotransmitter) and change it into another signal (metabolic or voltage changes in post synaptic neuron). Two important classes of receptors are ion channels and G-Protein coupled receptors.

receptor autoradiography A technique used to analyze the microscopic localization of drug and neurotransmitter receptors in slices of tissue.

reinforcement The period in which the drug user more frequently expresses drug-seeking behavior. It also consists of complex reactions to a drug that makes an organism repeat the drug taking and related actions.

salient   Novel and attention-grabbing.

sensitization   Occurs when repeated exposure with a stimulus leads to a greater response over time.

septum   An anatomical term for a wall or dividing structure. Also, a region in the forebrain.

signal transduction   The process of transmitting a signal from the outside to the inside of a cell. Also the process where stimulation of a neurotransmitter receptor results in the activation of intracellular, metabolic pathways, some of which can alter gene expression.

single nucleotide polymorphism   A common type of genetic variation in which one nucleotide is replaced with a different nucleotide in a stretch of DNA. In a population of individuals, some might have genes that differ from others by a single nucleotide.

synapse   A small junction between a nerve terminal and the following neuron. The neurotransmitter released from the nerve terminal must diffuse across this gap to act on receptors in the next postsynaptic neuron.

tolerance   Occurs when an increasingly larger amount of drug is required to achieve the same effect.

transcription factors   Molecules, typically proteins, which regulate gene expression by interacting with sites on the promoter region of a gene.

transporters   Proteins on neuronal membranes that pump neurotransmitters across the membrane from the outside to the inside of a nerve terminal.

variable number tandem repeat   A sequence of nucleotides that is repeated along a stretch of DNA a variable number of times.

ventral tegmental area   A brain structure that is part of the mesolimbic system and is associated with reward and reinforcement. It contains the cell bodies of dopaminergic neurons whose axons project to forebrain regions such as the nucleus accumbens.

vivarium   A contained area used for keeping laboratory animals.

vulnerability   The degree to which a person has a propensity to abuse drugs. There are both biological and environmental factors.

withdrawal   An unpleasant state that results from cessation of drug use. Depending on its severity and the drug involved, it can even be life threatening.

Index

classes of, 4-5
delivery methods, 53
dose-response studies, 37
harmful effects
    addictive properties versus,
      137-138
    of alcohol, 138-141
    of benzodiazepines, 148-149
    of caffeine, 152-153
    of club drugs, 150-151
    of cocaine, 145-146
    of marijuana, 143-144
    of methamphetamine, 146-148
    of nicotine, 141-143
    of opiates, 149-150
    of PCP, 151-152
legalization versus
  decriminalization, 198-200
legitimate uses for, 5
medications versus, 5
reasons for taking, 6
DSM IV TR (Diagnostic and
Statistical Manual of Mental
Disorders), 2, 13, 130

E

early life stress, drug use and,
  119-121
eating, dopamine and, 74-77
eating disorders
  as addiction, 130-132
  gene expression and, 76-77
Ecstasy, harmful effects of, 150-151
Edwards, Griffith, 202
Edwards, Roy, 95
elderly adults, drug addiction in, 167
electrical stimulation
  reinforcement, 29
    deep brain stimulation (DBS),
      33-34
    drug use and, 35-37
    food and water deprivation and, 34
    self-stimulation, 30-33
elephant and rider metaphor,
  110-112
emotional behavior, limbic system
  and, 10

emotional problems, vulnerability to
  drug use and, 106-107
emotional reactions to stress, 116
endogenous cannabinoids, 143
endorphins, morphine's effect on,
  51-52
enkephalins
  morphine's effect on, 51-52
  as neurotransmitters, 191
enriched environments, drug use
  and, 124-125
enzymes, defined, 41
epigenetics, 67-68, 191
epinephrine, 116
estrogen, effect on cocaine
  addiction, 161-163
excitatory signals, 42
excuse, addiction as, 133
exercise, as treatment, 178

F

family therapy, 178
finding treatment, resources for
  information, 184-186
Fitch, F., 192
Fleckenstein, Annette, 147
fMRI (functional magnetic
  resonance imaging), 12
food addiction, 130, 132
food deprivation, electrical
  stimulation reinforcement and, 34
food intake, dopamine and, 74-77
Fowler, Joanna, 95, 131
Francis, Darlene, 119
Freud, Sigmund, 111, 145
frontal cortex, 116, 164
frontal lobe, 10, 90, 165
functional magnetic resonance
  imaging (fMRI), 12
functions of brain regions, 10-11
future
  of addiction research, 191
  of treatment programs, 190
  of vaccines against drug abuse,
    192-194